D1482943

# MIGRATION POLICY IN EUROPE

# Migration Policy in Europe
# A Comparative Study

LEO H. KLAASSEN

and

PAUL DREWE

*Netherlands Economic Institute*

SAXON HOUSE | LEXINGTON BOOKS

*Published by*

SAXON HOUSE, D. C. Heath Ltd.
Westmead, Farnborough, Hants, England

*Jointly with*

LEXINGTON BOOKS, D. C. Heath & Co.
Lexington, Mass. U.S.A.

F. AS.

ISBN 0 347 01014 8
LC No. 72 14011
Printed in The Netherlands by D. Reidel Book Manufactures, Dordrecht

# Contents

# Appendix

# 0 An Introduction to Methodology and Concepts

## 0.1 The concept of mobility

### *0.1.1 Introduction*

Perfect mobility of the factors of production is a basic assumption of classical economic theory. It was assumed that even very small differences in the remuneration of labour or capital provided sufficient incentive to induce movement of workers and capital from the lower paid to the higher paid jobs. As a result of these induced movements, frictional differences in remuneration between sectors and regions disappeared immediately, so that even in the short run, no regional or sectoral differentials in wages or capital returns could exist.

With such a theory there is clearly no need for a special branch of regional economics or sectoral economics. If the marginal productivity of labour and of capital are the same in all branches, and basic economic forces tend to maintain this equilibrium, no individual sector or region requires special attention. The economy is permanently in an optimal situation.

In dynamic economic theory no such equilibrium exists. Significant economic and social obstacles to perfect mobility cause such time lags in the reactions of both workers and entrepreneurs that several regions and sectors may find themselves in a more or less permanent state of underemployment, even though some of the differences between regions and sectors are mitigated by a degree of mobility in factors of production to more favourable occupations.

It is the object of the mobility and migration policy of governments

a. to raise the mobility of labour and capital in general and

b. to provide incentives for people and industries that intend to move, and to those who have moved in so far as this move accords with the governments' regional targets. Industries are subsidised when they expand in designated areas and receive financial support for their loans and purchases of land and equipment.

Such measures are designed to make workers and entrepreneurs react more speedily and fully to existing differentials and to encourage those moves that serve national welfare targets and a balanced regional development. Since private economic considerations may differ from public social considerations, not *all* moves are receiving financial support, but only those that are thought to be in the national interest—where financial assistance is given to adjust the private economic and public social interests. Mobility policy is thus linked very closely with regional policy and special attention must be paid to these links whenever we study the measures taken by various governments to enhance the mobility of workers and entrepreneurs within the framework of a more general development policy. We start, however, by analysing somewhat more closely the concept of labour mobility.

## 0.1.2  Gross and net migration

Economic theory has tended to be concerned with net migration. It assumed that people were attracted by income differentials, acting to improve their own financial position (taking account of government aid). In this way they contribute not only to their own interest but also to the national interest.

In reality, however, people move not only for economic reasons but, perhaps even more, on social grounds. Family relationships, marriage, divorce, retirement etc., may all cause movements that are not related to economic or financial considerations. It is useful to examine this factor since it often arises when motives behind migration are discussed: it is often said that migrant surveys show that, for instance, income differentials play but a minor part in migration decisions.

In order to consider this aspect, we assume that three groups of factors play a role in explaining migration from region $i$ to region $j$. The first group constitutes the social relationships between regions $i$ and $j$. In principle the maximum number of such relationships between the two regions is given by the product of the numbers in the two populations. In practice, the number of relationships probably does not increase proportionally with that of possible relationships. We assume, therefore, that the actual number increases proportionally to the power $\alpha(\alpha < 1)$ of possible relationships, and that migration is proportional to actual relationships.

It is assumed that the second important factor is the income ratio between the region $i$ and the region $j$, the ratio $Y_j/Y_i$ where $Y_i$ is average income in region $i$. Whilst the employment situation might also play a role, we assume for simplicity's sake that the income factor represents both, since high income areas tend to have low unemployment.

The third factor, largely a psychological one, is distance. Although this partly represents the costs of moving and (more important) a lack of knowledge about conditions in the other region, it also embraces differences in 'environment' between the two regions, the degree of 'strangeness' increasing with the distance from the home region. These factors can be expressed in

2

a simple formula:

$$M_{ij} = \alpha_0 P_i^\alpha P_j^\alpha \left(\frac{Y_j}{Y_i}\right)^\beta e^{-\gamma A_{ij}} \tag{0.1}$$

in which $M_{ij}$=number of people migrating in a given period from region $i$ to region $j$.

$P_i$, $P_j$=population of regions $i$ and $j$ respectively.

$Y_i$, $Y_j$=average income in regions $i$ and $j$ respectively.

$A_{ij}$=distance between $i$ and $j$.

The expression for the flow of people migrating from $j$ to $i$ is:

$$M_{ji} = \alpha_0 P_i^\alpha P_j^\alpha \left(\frac{Y_i}{Y_j}\right)^\beta e^{-\gamma A_{ji}} \tag{0.2}$$

We now assume that $A_{ij}=A_{ji}$. This identity does not necessarily hold since the $A$'s represent psychological, not physical distances. With a city surrounded by an agricultural area, the psychological distance from the rural area of the average urban household might be different from that of the average rural household, from the city. We see later. however, that in general this assumption is valid so that it can be safely adopted at this stage.

The ratio of the number of people migrating from region $i$ to $j$ to those migrating from $j$ to $i$ is then given by:

$$\frac{M_{ij}}{M_{ji}} = \left(\frac{Y_j}{Y_i}\right)^{2\beta} \tag{0.3}$$

This ratio equals unity—there is no net migration—where $Y_j=Y_i$ and is larger (smaller) than unity where $Y_j$ is larger (smaller) than $Y_i$. Thus the size of net migration depends only upon the size of the income ratio between the regions.

From this simple analysis the following important conclusions may be drawn:

1. The results of surveys in which migrants are asked to state their motives for migration may only be used to identify those factors determining *gross* migration. No conclusions can be drawn from such surveys about the variables determining net migration.

2. The motives revealed by such surveys do not constitute sufficient information about the decision-making process of migrants, unless an average

3

weight is attached to each motive. Such weights could be found by a statistical analysis[1] of the survey results. In the above formulae these weights are represented by the exponents attached to the variables.

3. The influence of income on net migration is considerably larger than on gross migration, the coefficient of the income ratio in (0.3) being twice as large as those in (0.1) and (0.2).

### 0.1.3   The measurement of mobility

If the migration flow between regions in a given country is represented by equation (0.1):

$$M_{ij} = \alpha_0 (P_i P_j)^\alpha \left(\frac{Y_j}{Y_i}\right)^\beta e^{-\gamma A_{ij}}$$

the *mobility structure* of the population is described by the four coefficients $\alpha_0$, $\alpha$, $\beta$ and $\gamma$.

The coefficient $\alpha_0$ is a proportionality factor. The coefficients $\alpha$ and $\beta$ represent the influence of the population factors and income. Thus, if the income ratio for a given region is 1 per cent larger than for another, the number of migrants from the first region, other things being equal, will be $\beta$ per cent larger than from the second. Therefore, these coefficients are elasticities with respect to the two factors. The coefficient $\gamma$ is rather more difficult to interpret. Differentiating $M_{ij}$ with respect to $A_{ij}$ we find

$$\frac{\delta M_{ij}}{\delta A_{ij}} = -\gamma M_{ij} \tag{0.4}$$

and thus

$$\frac{\delta M_{ij}}{\delta A_{ij}} \cdot \frac{A_{ij}}{M_{ij}} = -\gamma A_{ij} \tag{0.5}$$

in which $-\gamma A_{ij}$ is the elasticity with respect to distance. It is zero for zero distance and increases proportionally with distance. That is, $\gamma$ represents the proportionality factor with which the distance elasticity increases with distance. Evidently the value of all three coefficients may lie within a wide range, which for $\alpha$ runs from zero to one and for $\beta$ and $\gamma$ comprises all positive values.

It follows from the foregoing, that the number of migrants can never be used as an indication of the mobility of a given population, since it is a number which results from the structure of mobility (the coefficients) as well as the intensities of the incentives (variables).

It is important not to lose sight of this. If, for instance, the coefficients of the distance factor are the same in two regions, then the number of people moving from these two regions, lying at distances of 50 and 100 km respectively from a third region to that third region (all other factors equal) will differ, the number migrating from the second region being much smaller than that from the first region. Yet, the mobility of the populations in the two regions is exactly the same, only the intensity of the incentives varies. The importance of distance as an obstacle to migration is identical for the populations of both regions. The distance itself, however, differs.

These considerations yield an important conclusion, namely that it can only be claimed that the mobility of the population in country I is larger than in country II, if—and only if—all coefficients in (0.1) are larger in country I than in country II. In all other cases such a general conclusion may not be drawn, and statements should be limited to comparisons of the individual elasticities of migration with respect to a specific explanatory variable or to the intrinsic mobility. It follows that conclusions about the level or structure of mobility in a given country can never be reached only on the basis of the number of migrants. This number of migrants is determined by the structure of mobility ($\alpha_0$, $\alpha$, $\beta$ and $\gamma$) together with the values of the incentives ($P_i P_j$, $Y_j/Y_i$ and $A_{ij}$). Such statements as 'Americans are more mobile than Europeans' should therefore be regarded with scepticism, as long as information about all the coefficients is missing. Mere numbers are insufficient.

This principle can be demonstrated in mathematical terms if we write

$$m_{ij}^{(1)} = m_{ij}^{(1)}(\alpha^{(1)}, \mathbf{x}^{(1)})$$

and

$$m_{ij}^{(2)} = m_{ij}^{(2)}(\alpha^{(2)}, \mathbf{x}^{(2)})$$

where $\alpha$ is the vector of coefficients and $\mathbf{x}$ that of the variables, for the migration flows in countries 1 and 2 respectively. The ratio of mobility in the two countries is then defined as the ratio of the number of migrants for a *standardised* set of the variables, i.e. as

$$\mu = \frac{m_{ij}^{(1)}(\alpha^{(1)}, \bar{\mathbf{x}})}{m_{ij}^{(2)}(\alpha^{(2)}, \bar{\mathbf{x}})} = \mu(\alpha^{(1)}, \alpha^{(2)}, \bar{\mathbf{x}})$$

Only for those values of the $\alpha$'s and $\mathbf{x}$ for which $\mu > 1$ can it be said that mobility in country 1 is greater than in country 2. It follows that it is possible (and later we see examples of this phenomenon) that for *some* values of $\mathbf{x}$, $\mu > 1$ but for others $\mu < 1$. A country might have a high mobility for short distances and a low mobility for long distances.

Another example illustrates this principle. Assume the following equations

5

for inter-regional migration hold in countries A and B respectively:

$$M_A = \alpha_0 \, (P_i P_j)^{0.75} \left(\frac{Y_j}{Y_i}\right)^{1.0} e^{-\gamma A} \tag{0.6}$$

$$M_B = \alpha_0 \, (P_i P_j)^{0.75} \left(\frac{Y_j}{Y_i}\right)^{0.5} e^{-\gamma A} \tag{0.7}$$

Since the proportionality factors ($\alpha_0$) as well as the coefficients of $P_i P_j$ and $A_{ij}$ are identical, but the value of the coefficient of $Y_j/Y_i$ in country A is double that in country B, mobility in A is greater than in B. Assume, however, that country A consists of two regions with an income differential of 10 per cent and country B of two regions with a differential of 44 per cent, so that $Y_j/Y_i = 1.1$ in country A and $(Y_j/Y_i)^{0.5} = 1.2$ in country B. If all other factors were equal, the number of migrants in B would be 10 per cent larger than in A, despite the fact that mobility in B is less than in A. Again, the example serves to emphasise what great care is needed when referring to the mobility of a population. In general it is more prudent to limit statements to the proportionality factor and the partial mobilities represented by the coefficients in the equations.

Consequently, when evaluating the effectiveness of government aids to labour mobility, ideally a sharp distinction should be drawn between, on the one hand, the incentives offered and on the other the efforts to increase the influence of a given incentive. The former measures constitute a migration policy, and as such are largely short run, the second kind of measure represents a long term mobility policy. Whilst the word migration, not mobility, appears in the title of this study, we should remember that it is concerned both with government migration policy and mobility policy.

### 0.1.4  Qualification of the population variables

No allowance has yet been made for the fact that certain groups in the population are considerably more mobile than others. The young, as well as the better educated, are assumed (an assumption considered later) to react faster than the elderly and less educated. A statistical problem arises because the young tend to be better educated, so that, at least in macro-analysis, it is often difficult to separate the influences of the two factors. For purposes of forecasting, this difficulty is not too serious, but it proves more troublesome for mobility policy, since education levels can be influenced but age distribution cannot. The consequences of this difference in mobility between age groups will later be considered by substituting the younger population for the total population.

A second qualification can be introduced to the population variable in the receiving area. It seems logical—and symmetrical to the considerations set forth in the preceding paragraph—not to examine all possible relationships with region $j$ but only those that are important for the younger people from region $i$. For this purpose existing employment in manufacturing and service growth-industries will be later introduced. It should be recognised that in the process we eliminate income as a separate variable, so far as income differentials between regions stem from differences in sectoral structures.

## 0.2  A mobility policy

### 0.2.1  General

The general objective of mobility policy is to make people react more sharply to stimulants that are likely to improve their socio-economic position. This means that measures which tend to raise mobility with respect to social factors are relevant to a mobility policy only in so far as they also increase economic mobility.

Using terms formulated in the previous section, it follows that the object of a mobility policy is to influence the value of the coefficients in the equation which explains the level of migration. More precisely, the objective is to raise the positive value of the income elasticity and to lower the negative value of the distance coefficient.

In order to be more specific let us consider the decision of a person contemplating migration from region $i$ to region $j$. In this three elements play a role in his decision: (a) the advantages and disadvantages of remaining in region $i$; (b) the advantages and disadvantages of working and living in region $j$; (c) the cost involved in moving from $i$ to $j$. In his decision-making process, the potential migrant will evaluate simultaneously the factors under (a) and (b), draw up a balance of net advantages and net disadvantages and compare it with the cost involved in moving.

Such a procedure approaches very closely a private cost–benefit analysis, but there are some basic differences of which the migration policy must take account if it is not to be unrealistic. With a 'normal' cost–benefit analysis, future income flows, as well as costs, are expressed in current value by discounting with the prevailing long term interest rate. A subjective cost–benefit analysis differs in two respects from this procedure.

Firstly, the information available to an inhabitant of region $i$ about most other regions is defective, incomplete and vague. He is usually ill-informed about wage rates, rents, school fees and other prices, and in consequence will undertake his calculations with a large degree of uncertainty. If he overestimates certain advantages he might undertake the move, become disenchanted and return quickly to his home region. Should he underestimate advantages, he might not move at all. In both cases the lack of factual knowledge leads to a wrong decision.

Secondly, the long-run benefits of a move will be underestimated since calculations based on subjective interest rates lead to a relative overestimation of current welfare and an underestimation of possible future net improvements. Although no precise information is available, it can be assumed that subjective interest rates are considerably higher than actual ones. The same consideration is conducive to an underestimation of the benefits that a migrant's children might experience in a later period. These aspects of migration are examined more fully in Chapter 3.

In the light of such considerations we might reformulate the objectives of a mobility policy, so that it is regarded as the complex of measures that brings individual subjective cost–benefit calculations as near as possible to the objective ones—as well as giving assistance during the preparation and transition period in so far as it seems desirable, to those who actually move.

This formulation yields the basic elements of a mobility policy. They are:

1. To raise the general educational level, particularly in regions where it is below average. A higher educational level not only directly improves knowledge about other regions but also it is conducive to better judgements about the opportunities which exist elsewhere. Although this effect belongs as much in the domain of educational as mobility policy, it is mentioned here because of its general significance particularly for the most immobile groups of the population.

2. To improve the dispersion of information about specific opportunities in expanding regions. Measures in this category might range from the provision of simple written information about future job opportunities and vacancies, to informative evenings and journeys to other regions. It is well known that an absence of information about other regions is a major obstacle to migration.

Such a mobility policy will usually lead to better, more rational, decisions by people contemplating a move from one region to another. In order to reconcile the decisions with national targets for balanced regional growth, that is in order to render private economic decisions compatible with national economic goals, three major groups of instruments can be used: improvements in the skills of potential migrants and their adjustment to the needs of the expanding regions; financial assistance with the costs of moving; housing programmes in the receiving regions which facilitate the move. The latter point is of considerable importance since expanding regions are usually those with a housing deficit so that the conditions in which immigrants live, at least initially are frequently rather primitive.

The two elements listed above, which constitute a mobility policy, contribute to a better understanding and judgement of opportunities elsewhere, by promoting right decisions and minimising wrong ones. The other three elements of a migration policy facilitate the process of transition once a decision in principle to migrate has been taken on the basis of available knowledge and information, and also influence the decision in the desired direction from a socio-economic viewpoint.

This study is concerned with the financial assistance element of migration policy, although other elements of mobility and migration policy will be touched upon.

### 0.2.2   *Motives and barriers*

It is useful, at this stage, to introduce two concepts which will be treated in depth in Chapter 1, but which are also connected with the preceding discussion. In Chapter 1 the concepts, motives for and barriers to migration are introduced. For convenience we use only 'motive' here, considering a barrier simply as a negative motive. For any individual each motive has a certain intensity and a subjective average weight that he attaches to this intensity. For instance, he might consider as a motive a certain income differential, but he must attach a weight to this sum in order to evaluate its importance in relation to other motives. The decision whether or not to migrate therefore depends upon the outcome of a comparison of weighted motives (and barriers).

Let us denote the intensity of motive $i$ by $m_i$ and the weight attached to it by $w_i$. As it seems likely that $w_i$ will vary between different groups in the population and between regions, we will consider the case of a homogeneous group in a given region for which $w_i$ is the same for each individual.[2]

The expected 'profit' of migration for the individual $k$ thus equals

$$\pi_k = \sum_i m_{ki} w_i \tag{0.8}$$

In (0.8) a subscript $ki$ is attached to the motives to indicate that the intensity of each motive is basically a matter of personal judgement and based upon vague and insufficient knowledge for many individuals. Each individual has ideas about the conditions under which he would be able to work and live in another region and possibly also in another job. The knowledge on which this idea is based is however incomplete and, above all, differs from individual to individual. We will assume, however, that the *average* estimate of all the individuals for each motive is right. This means that we will assume a frequency distribution of estimates of intensities of motives of which the mean coincides with the actual value. In other words, we put forward the hypothesis that the average of all individual estimates about incomes to be earned elsewhere coincides with the actual income there.

This assumption can be expressed as

$$\text{var}\,(m_{ki}) = \sigma_i^2 \tag{0.9}$$

and

$$E(m_{ki}) = m_i \tag{0.10}$$

It follows that the variance of the distribution of $\pi_k$ equals

$$\text{var}\,(\pi_k) = \sum_i \sigma_i^2 w_i^2 = \sigma^2 \tag{0.11}$$

and

$$E(\pi_k) = \pi \tag{0.12}$$

in which $\pi$ is the realised profit after migration.

We now assume that everybody emigrates for whom $\pi_k > s$, that is for whom the expected profit to be obtained from emigration exceeds a certain critical level $s$. If in fact $s$ exceeds $\pi$, in other words if

$$s = \pi + \alpha\sigma \quad \text{where} \quad (\alpha > 0) \tag{0.13}$$

all those for whom $\pi_k > s$ decide wrongly to emigrate. Clearly, given $s$, $\alpha$ will be larger the smaller $\sigma$ is, which means that the better the judgement of opportunities elsewhere, the smaller the number of individuals who make a wrong decision.

If we now assume that $s$ is smaller than $\pi$, in other words

$$s = \pi - \alpha\sigma \quad (\alpha > 0) \tag{0.14}$$

all those for whom $\pi_k > s$ decide wrongly, not to emigrate. Their number also decreases with a decrease in $\sigma$. In this case $\alpha$ increases and consequently a smaller number will take the wrong decision not to emigrate.

If we call the wrong decision in the latter case an error of type II and the wrong decision in the former case an error of type I[3] we may draw up Table 0.1.

Table 0.1.

| Decision | In reality, migration | |
|---|---|---|
| | not justified | justified |
| No migration | Decision correct | Type II error |
| Migration | Type I error | Decision correct |

It follows from the analysis above that numbers of people making errors of type I as well as of type II will be reduced if $\sigma$ is reduced. Since $\sigma$ represents a lack of information as well as imperfect judgement both elements of *mobility policy*—the provision of more and better education by which the judgement is improved over the long term, and providing more and better information to strengthen the *basis for judgement* during the short term—may help considerably to avoid wrong decisions and promote right ones.

The effect of accentuating the intensities of migration motives or, in other words, increasing the importance of incentives and decreasing the importance of barriers, can be shown in the following way. Let us assume that a migration subsidy is only justified if the decision to migrate (taking the subsidy into consideration) is justified from a national economic viewpoint. Clearly, if this were not the case, the subsidisation of a move would only result in a larger number of wrong decisions (type I error) and thus have an adverse effect. If the move is justified, however, the subsidy raises the number of correct decisions to migrate at the expense of the number of wrong decisions not to migrate. This discussion can be illuminated by some graphs. First, the effect can be demonstrated of a mobility policy which decreases the size of the standard deviation of the frequency distribution of potential migrants according to their expected profits from migration ($\pi_k$).

The original distribution is that shown in Graph 0.1

The shaded area represents the number of people who wrongly emigrated. Their expected profit from the migration $\pi_k > s$ exceeded $\pi$, which means that they overestimated the advantages of migration. Better information and improved judgement would reduce the variance of the distribution, changing it into the one shown in Graph 0.2.

Because of the smaller variance the shaded area has decreased considerably in size, which means a reduction in the number of individuals making an

Graph 0.1

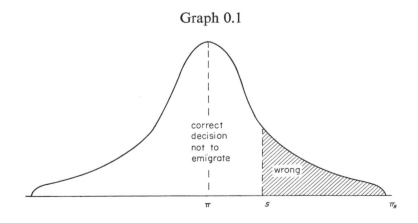

11

error of type I. Where actual profit from migration exceeds the critical level, the situation is as depicted in Graph 0.3.

This graph changes as the previous case into Graph 0.4.

Here, again the number of correct decisions rises and the number of type II errors falls.

The effects of migration policy can be shown in a similar fashion. First it can be shown that where the emigration (again, after subsidisation) is *not*

Graph 0.2

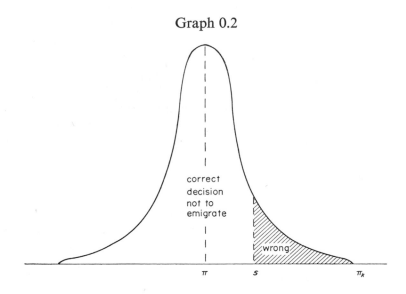

Graph 0.3

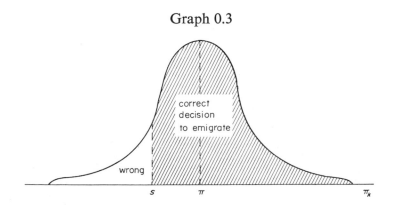

## Graph 0.4

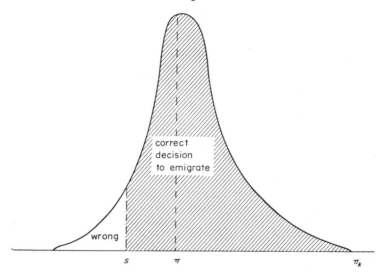

## Graph 0.5

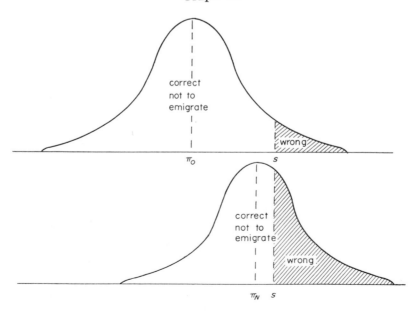

justified, migration aid tends to increase the number of people making type I errors (emigration where it is not justified). It is assumed that the individual is aware of the subsidy available to him.

See Graph 0.5 in which
$$\pi_N - \pi_0 = S. \tag{0.15}$$

The 'profit' to be obtained from migration without subsidy is indicated by $\pi_0$ and with subsidy by $\pi_N$. It is clear that the number of wrong decisions is positively influenced by the migration subsidy, so that the number of type I errors increases. Evidently migration policy needs to be implemented very carefully in order to avoid this effect.

The number of type II errors always decreases as a result of migration policy. This is shown in Graph 0.6.

In this case the subsidy $(\pi_N - \pi_0)$ has a favourable influence, helping individuals to avoid type II errors.

In the following, an attempt is made to draw a sharp distinction between mobility policy (although such a policy might not explicitly exist) and migration policy. Mobility is the propensity to migrate, migration is the decision itself. Even the very mobile may never, in fact, move.

### 0.2.3 Selective migration policy

We have already stipulated that migration policy seeks to stimulate move-

Graph 0.6

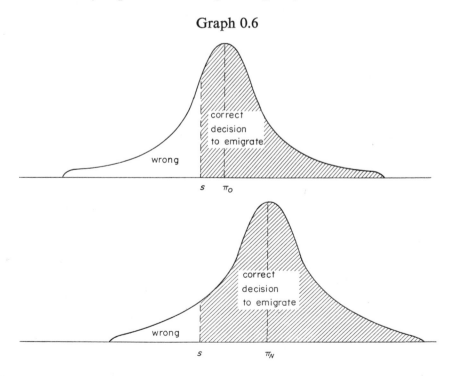

ments between regions, often associated with a change in occupation made possible by adjusting the workers' skills to the needs of the receiving region. Basically this implies: (a) that some regions are considered as potential expulsion regions and others as potential absorbing regions; and (b) that some sectors are regarded as stagnating and others as expanding; and (c) it is thought desirable that workers move between those sectors and regions.

Although this aspect is examined in more detail in the next section, it seems appropriate at this stage to indicate the relations that exist between regional policies in some countries and their migration policies. In certain countries migration policy and migration studies are focused upon specific population groups and on particular regions. The policy identifies which groups should migrate, as well as the regions between which they should move, and in this way the purposes of the regional policy are served.

Although migration and regional policies should always be consistent and provide mutual support, their reconciliation—which in practice consists of adjusting migration policy to regional policy—can be meaningless if the regional policy is internally inconsistent, a phenomenon which is anything but rare. If areas are designated as development areas, but in fact have no future at all, a migration policy which attempts to move people to these areas or prevents emigration from them, will only exacerbate the areas' difficulties. If therefore migration policy is to be selective, it should realistically be so and, if necessary, regional objectives should be ignored if unlikely to meet with much success. The following section develops this theme in more detail.

## 0.3  Mobility policy and regional policy

### 0.3.1  Introduction

Regional policies in Europe are usually based on the growth-pole principle.[4] This means that those regions whose development is to be stimulated are not helped in their entirety but the measures taken are focused on a limited number of nuclei within their boundaries. It is hoped that once these nuclei have reached a minimum size, a process of self-sustaining growth will start. Regions with the highest unemployment rates and lowest *per capita* incomes are usually chosen for development.

Quite often the regional policy contains another element, namely a limitation on the development of the largest cities, since their growth is considered to be at the expense of the smaller centres. Sometimes both elements are united in an attempt to divert activities from over-large cities directly to the development areas. In linking both objectives of regional policy in this way an effort is made to achieve more acceptable regional income differentials as quickly as possible.

It cannot be claimed that this kind of regional policy has hitherto been very

15

effective. The reason for this is not difficult to trace. Areas designated as development areas are usually the most difficult to develop, while the development of large cities is most difficult to stop. Moreover, the choice of nuclei within development areas is often heavily influenced by political pressures, which leads to the designation of too many nuclei, thereby not only weakening the impact of designation, but also yielding less growth than a smaller number of nuclei might have achieved. In consequence, regional development in many European countries (and in the United States) is not much influenced by regional policy, and there continues to be a concentration in those areas already highly urbanised.

In these circumstances a migration policy which seeks to induce a population movement towards the development nuclei makes very little sense. If demand for labour in these nuclei does not significantly increase, there is not much point in increasing the supply of workers.

### 0.3.2 A labour market model

The problems involved can best be demonstrated by a simple model, consisting of four equations:

$$\frac{\Delta L_S}{L_S} = \pi + \frac{M_L}{L_S} \tag{0.16}$$

$$\frac{M_L}{L_S} = \alpha \frac{Y - \bar{Y}}{\bar{Y}} - \alpha\sigma_L \tag{0.17}$$

$$\frac{\Delta L_D}{L_D} = -\beta \frac{Y - \bar{Y}}{\bar{Y}} + \beta\sigma_C + \xi \tag{0.18}$$

$$\frac{\Delta L_D}{L_D} = \frac{\Delta L_S}{L_S} \tag{0.19}$$

Equation (0.16) shows that the rise in labour supply, in a given region, comprises the natural net increase $\pi$ plus the migration rate. Equation (0.17) indicates that the rate of net migration varies with the deviation of the region's average real income from the national average, and on the relative size of the government support to migrants presented on an annual basis ($\sigma = S_L/Y$, in which $S_L$ is the absolute amount of support, also shown annually).

It appears that the term $\alpha\sigma_L$ can be interpreted in two ways. If the authorities support migration towards more developed areas, $\sigma_L > 0$ for migration from the underdeveloped regions ($Y < \bar{Y}$), and $\sigma_L = 0$ for migration from the developed regions ($Y > \bar{Y}$). Swedish policy is of this kind, stimulating a movement from poorer to richer regions.

Where the government encourages migration to development regions, or

16

rather discourages emigration from these regions, in support of efforts to industrialise them by subsidising industry locating there, then $\sigma_L > 0$ for the migration to underdeveloped regions and $\sigma_L = 0$ for migration to developed regions. This policy is, roughly speaking, the one pursued in the Netherlands and France.

Equation (0.18) represents the demand for labour. It indicates that a rise in labour demand depends on the deviation of the region's average wage from the national average, on the government subsidy to locating and expanding industries (expressed as an annual figure per worker employed), and the autonomous growth of labour demand in the region (which is determined by the specific economic structure of the region). Equation (0.19) is an equilibrium relation, in which it is assumed that the relative increase in demand equals the relative increase in supply.

In Equations (0.17) and (0.18), coefficients $\alpha$ and $\beta$ represent, respectively, the mobility of labour and capital (the demand for labour). Coefficient $\alpha$ reflects the degree to which workers react to financial incentives and $\beta$ the degree to which industries respond to wage differentials. The latter variable is used for the wage level and *per capita* income.

We refer to a policy that seeks to influence the value of $\alpha$ as a labour mobility policy and one that tries to affect $\beta$ as a capital mobility policy. A policy using $\sigma_L$ as an instrument for influencing the migration of workers is termed a migration policy, and one that uses $\sigma_C$ as an instrument, a regional policy. If the model is solved for the exogenous (including instrument) variables, we obtain four equations:

$$\frac{Y-\bar{Y}}{Y} = \frac{1}{\alpha+\beta}\,(\xi-\pi) + \frac{\alpha}{\alpha+\beta}\,\sigma_L + \frac{\alpha}{\alpha+\beta}\,\sigma_C \tag{0.20}$$

$$\frac{M_L}{L_S} = \frac{\alpha}{\alpha+\beta}\,(\xi-\pi) + \frac{\alpha\beta}{\alpha+\beta}\,(\sigma_C-\sigma_L) \tag{0.21}$$

$$\frac{\Delta L_D}{L_D} = \frac{\Delta L_S}{L_S} = \frac{\alpha}{\alpha+\beta}\,\xi + \frac{\beta}{\alpha+\beta}\,\pi + \frac{\alpha\beta}{\alpha+\beta}\,(\sigma_C-\sigma_L). \tag{0.22}$$

For our purpose the most important are Equations (0.20) and (0.21). Equation (0.20) shows that the income level in the region is influenced by the discrepancy between the autonomous growth of labour demand and the natural rate of increase of the working population, as well as by subsidies on labour and capital movements. The impact of the first of these factors decreases with greater mobility of labour and capital. The effect of migration policy $(\alpha/\alpha+\beta)$ increases with labour mobility, and that of regional policy rises with capital mobility.

The interpretation to be attached to Equation (0.20) varies with the kind of regional policy pursued. If the policy is one of support to migrants from underdeveloped regions and to industries locating there, but excludes support to workers and capital migrating from the developed regions, the equation applies to underdeveloped regions only. In this case, $\sigma_C$ helps in narrowing the regional income differentials and $\sigma_L$ also contributes towards this. If the policy supports immigration into the underdeveloped areas, as in the Netherlands and France, Equation (0.20) needs to be interpreted differently. In this case $\sigma_L$ operates as a negative factor, counteracting the influence of $\sigma_C$ and retarding the equalisation of incomes. From Equation (0.21) it can be seen that such a subsidy decreases total migration, supporting a regional policy which has the same effect.

If attention is focused specifically on migration policy, that is using $\sigma_L$ as an instrument variable, and if the equalisation of regional incomes is adopted as the goal, the following conclusions emerge.

1. The impact of a migration policy in a region with a relatively low income level is more favourable as the mobility of its population rises.

2. A regional policy, pursued simultaneously, enhances the impact of migration policy on income if, and only if, the migration policy seeks to stimulate emigration out of underdeveloped regions. If its objective is to retard emigration from underdeveloped regions, the two policies have opposite effects on income.

The first conclusion implies that high mobility is an essential condition for a successful migration policy. Mobility policy is the instrument which does most to enhance effectiveness of migration policy. If mobility cannot be increased at short notice for the region in question (which is very likely), a regional policy might be more effective.

### 0.3.3 Consistent regional and migration policies

In most countries a regional industrialisation policy and a migration policy are simultaneously implemented. In the light of the contents of the previous section, the question is posed: to what extent can a regional industrialisation policy and a migration policy be combined in a consistent manner to attain given targets as quickly as possible? The same section provided a first answer to this question.

It is useful to pose a further question: how often are measures embraced by a regional industrialisation policy for stimulating the growth of certain underdeveloped regions, taken independently of 'development-worthiness' of that region (represented by $\xi$ in our model)? The answer to this question is,

18

frequently. The reasons for this are usually political in nature, and on the same grounds the view that emigration from the region might help more than anything else, is very seldom defended. Still, the object of regional policy is to ensure that *the people* in a particular region are provided with a good job as quickly as possible—preferably in their own region, but if this is difficult, then in another one. The first object should always be to help people, and through them the region.

If a region's industrial development potential is good, jobs should be brought to people; if it is not, people should be brought to places where jobs exist. The basis for such a policy should be the designation of growth poles (development nuclei) in places where there is a sound potential for future development, and, consequently, where success can be envisaged for the necessary measures.

The selection of restricted number of such potentially favourable growth poles implies a twofold decision: the designation of immigration areas where the autonomous growth of industry is to be deliberately stimulated and, simultaneously, a decision that a number of other areas, not designated as development areas, should be regarded as out-migration areas. The latter decision may not be very easy, but it is a necessary complement to the first. Industry development in the selected growth centres will be stimulated by financial assistance to industries moving to or expanding in those centres, while out-migration from the areas that are not supported would be facilitated by measures taken in the framework of the geographic labour mobility policy. Entrepreneurs and workers alike, would benefit from such a policy and contribute towards its success.

## 0.3.4  *The consequence of out-migration*

To conclude the introduction, attention needs to be paid to an argument that is often brought up when considering the consequences of out-migration on the quality of the labour force. It is alleged that, whenever out-migration occurs from an area, the younger and more active people leave and development prospects deteriorate, in consequence. In fact, a similar argument can be applied to stagnating sectors. In their case slow development would induce the younger and more active to leave, thus worsening the sector's future prospects.

The argument lacks precision in two ways. Firstly, this view appears to be more concerned with regions than people. If people can improve their lot by moving out of an area, they should do so. One might argue that it is the duty of the authorities to help them to do so, even to the point where they are educated for this purpose.

It might be stated, in reply, that a basic objective of regional policy is to develop each area and that possession of a stock of well-trained young people is a necessary condition for such development: if these people were to leave the area, further growth would be endangered and their out-migration should therefore be prevented. This leads to the second weakness of the argument: the implicit assumption that the stock of skilled young people is constant so that each migrant decreases its size. In reality, particularly in many under-developed areas, the natural growth of population is considerable, so that the young people form a relatively large part of the community. Even agricultural areas, with high emigration rates, usually display a population age-distribution considerably more 'favourable' in this respect than that of urbanised and industrial areas where natural growth is much lower. This implies that agricultural areas can afford to lose a considerable number of young people without endangering in the least the stock of young and skilled workers. As a result, in so far as it is valid that the young and skilled are an important prerequisite for future growth (there is not much supporting evidence for this assumption since development is often slowest in areas where population growth is high) the argument should at least be reformulated to require only that the emigration of the young and skilled ought not to be excessive in comparison with the natural growth of their number.

There is another factor too. The argument states that young and skilled people should stay in their area for the sake of its future development: in short, their value to the area should be calculated not on their present contribution to the area's income but, much more, on their future contribution. If the latter is, in fact larger than the former, they should be compensated accordingly to prevent their movement. As long as this is not done, the decision of the individual who can improve his position by emigrating is perfectly rational, and contributes to the country's welfare as well as to his own.

### Notes

1 See H. Emanuel, L. H. Klaassen and H. Theil, 'On the interactions of purchasing motives and the optimal programming of their activation', *Management Science*, 7 October 1960; 62–79.

2 The analysis can easily be extended to the case in which $w_i$ also differs between individuals.

3 The usual statistical practice.

4 Great Britain is an exception.

# 1 Forms of Geographical Labour Migration

Definitions of geographical labour mobility are as numerous as studies of this phenomenon.[1] To avoid conceptional confusion the particular phenomena of immediate interest need to be classified. Our topic is the process of members of the labour force (and their dependents) moving from one region to another, changing their residence and place of work. Strictly, this definition is one of geographical labour migration. As stated, 'migration' refers to a form of *behaviour*, whilst 'mobility' refers to an *attitude* to movement, the propensity to move. It is necessary to emphasise this distinction because uncritical use of these terms could introduce a fundamental confusion into the discussion and analysis. The labour markets corresponding to our definition of geographical labour migration are the regional sub-markets. Although external migration is excluded from this study, it should be remembered that this phenomenon is increasing in relative importance alongside the progressive integration of economies. In addition to inter-regional migration, two other forms of geographical labour migration are pertinent in the context of local labour markets: changes of residence and job location within a region; and daily commuting between residence and workplace. In metropolitan areas especially there is a growing tendency either to change only one's job location or to change only residence (residential migration), movements which tend to happen within the local labour market area. Both these forms of geographical labour migration generate commuting. The most significant criterion on which to draw a distinction between local and regional labour markets is distance—physical, or even better economic (using travel costs and intervening economic opportunities) and social distance (communication barriers and travel times).

Within a short radius [2] from home, commuting can substitute for migration so that a job location can be changed without change of residence. At greater distances from home, places of work can be changed only when the residence is changed. It then depends on the demarcation of regions whether a move has to be classified as intra- or inter-regional labour migration.

There are no general rules about defining regions. Illustrations of a pragmatic approach will be given later. Regional demarcation should be meaningful in the context of the country studied and practical for the purpose of studying basic features of inter-regional labour migration. This topic will be considered from the point of view of active manpower policy.

Intra-regional labour migration has a manpower interest, too, but on a smaller geographical scale. However commuting, and separate changes in job location and (especially) residential location, are of primary interest to city and transportation planners.

Table 1.1 provides a summary classification of forms of geographical labour migration.

Table 1.1.

Forms of Internal Geographical Migration

| Job location | | Residence | | |
|---|---|---|---|---|
| | | No change | Change | |
| | No change | (Commuting) | ← Residential migration | |
| | | ↑ | | |
| | | ⏐ | | |
| | Change | Change of job location | Intra-regional migration | Inter-regional migration |
| | | Regional* | | National† |
| | | ............... Labour market | | .............. |

\* The local sub-markets of a region
† The regional sub-markets of the nation.

## 1.2 Inter-regional labour migration as a decision-making process

### 1.2.1 Motives and barriers

In order to understand the factors influencing inter-regional migration, it is useful to regard a move as the result of a decision-making process.[3] Before individuals and households finally engage in the adventure of changing their whole social environment (workplace, residence, educational and recreational facilities etc.) many occurrences take place, usually simultaneously although the elements relevant to the decision can be described for illustrative purposes in form of a sequence (Table 1.2). First, the decision has to be made to abandon an old place. The reason for such a decision may be dissatisfaction with existing working and housing conditions. Sometimes the decision to leave may be forced by external circumstances. During the second stage, the search for a new place, channels of information and ideal requirements (that is the desired features of the new workplace and residence) play a role. During the third stage, a selection is made from alternative choices. In some circumstances there may effectively be only a single alternative work and dwelling opportunity.

Table 1.2.

Stages in Decision-making

| Stage I | Stage II | Stage III |
|---|---|---|
| The decision to abandon an old residence and job location | The search for a new residence and location | The choice among alternative new residences and job locations |
| *Reasons for changing:* | *Relevant considerations:* | *Reasons for choice:* |
| A. Decision forced by external circumstances | A. *Channels of information* | A. Only one alternative offered: attractions presumed to be identical with specifications |
| B. Decision made because of dissatisfaction with old residence and job location (*complaints*) | B. *Specifications* (desired features of new residence and job location) | B. Several possibilities: choice on grounds of comparative *attractions* of alternatives |

Source: Rossi, op. cit. p. 174.

It follows from the scheme presented in Table 1.2 that there are at least four different types of move that can be distinguished, according to the way in which each of the elements of the scheme are involved. As Table 1.3 shows, apart from full moves (I), there are those with constraints on choice among new residences and job locations (II), those of people satisfied with their old place (III) and those of people without a choice (IV).

Statistics which merely measure the total number of migrants from a certain origin to a certain destination comprise all four types of move in this classification. The evidence available is not usually directly related to inter-regional labour migration, and a distinction is only normally made between 'free choice' and 'forced moves'. Nevertheless it can be useful to consider such evidence when migration statistics are being interpreted and when policy measures to influence migration are discussed.[4]

It was found that out of a total of 444 residential moves in Philadelphia 51 per cent were in the free choice category while 39 per cent were forced, including involuntary moves as a result of evictions, dwelling destruction

Table 1.3.

Classification of Inter-regional Labour Moves

| Move type | Involving | | | |
| --- | --- | --- | --- | --- |
| | Complaints? | Information Sources? | Specifications? | Attractions? |
| I. Full Choice Moves | Yes | Yes | Yes | Yes |
| II. Dissatisfied, No Choice Moves | Yes | Yes | Yes | No |
| III. Forced, Full Choice Moves | No | Yes | Yes | Yes |
| IV. Forced, No Choice Moves | No | Yes | Yes | No |

Source: Rossi, op, cit. p. 129.

and severe income loss.[5] Rundblad found for Norrköping 'that about 25 per cent of the changes in the oldest age group were 'forced moves', for example caused by layoff, compared with 19 per cent in the middle age group and 18 per cent in the youngest age group.'[6]

Up to this point we have considered only complete decisions, that is decisions that lead, in some way, to action, to movement. However, it may be more important for formulating migration policy to know something about incomplete decisions. By this we mean situations where dissatisfaction is aroused by work and dwelling conditions in a given location but where this dissatisfaction cannot manifest itself in a move. Incomplete decisions imply the existence of barriers against migration. There is no barrier problem in the case of forced moves. With more or less free moves, there is, on one hand, dissatisfaction with the old work and residence—complaints and notions about the ideal features of potential new jobs and residences testify to this. But, on the other, there is the question whether the individual or household, frustrated in some way, decides to abandon a former residence and job to search for new locations and finally makes a choice between them—or at least takes the only opportunity that exists. Such decisions will not be made and consequent actions will not be taken, where certain barriers are effective.

With a given set of 'complaints' and 'specifications' no opportunities at all may exist. For instance, a Dutch miner, unemployed because of the closure of mines in Limburg, will be faced with a complete lack of alternative opportunities if he wants to continue as a miner and in the Netherlands. It is clear that opportunities in this sense are *apparent* opportunities, that is opportunities as judged by the individual or household involved, according to the 'complaints' and 'specifications'. Such apparent opportunities do not necessarily coincide with objective opportunities—opportunities in the eyes of an 'outsider', a civil servant or politician.[7] A second kind of barrier may result from the absence of, or inadequate, information about existing opportunities available to individuals and households. In more general terms, it is clear that adequate channels of information require more than mere knowledge about jobs or housing in new locations: since inter-regional labour migration implies a change of the whole social milieu, more is required—it might be termed channels of communication—as will be explained below in some detail. But even if some (or at least one) apparent opportunities exist, implying that there is adequate information or communication, potential movers may still be unable to move. Such capability barriers can consist of three major components.

A move costs money so that barriers may exist because of deficiencies in financial resources. Ill-health constitutes another kind of barrier. Finally, social inadequacies may make it difficult to cope with some moves to more satisfying jobs and residences. Inter-regional labour mobility, using this phrase in its attitudinal sense, is only a specific case of a more general social problem that occurs every time an individual is required to make a new choice.

Inter-regional labour migration is the adoption of an innovation which requires a general readiness to accept change.[8] In our special case, it may be called mobility-mindedness. The place of the various barriers in the decision-making process can be identified in Table 1.4.

Table 1.4.

Incomplete Decisions and Types of Barriers

| Barriers resulting from lack or inadequacy of: | Com-plaints? | Specifi-cations? | Capa-bility? | Inform-ation? | Attrac-tion(s)? |
|---|---|---|---|---|---|
| I.   Opportunities | Yes | Yes | Yes | Yes | No |
| II.  Information | Yes | Yes | Yes | No | No |
| III. Capability (physical, financial, social) | Yes | Yes | No | Yes | Yes |

### 1.2.2 The motives specified

It follows from the decision-making process described that the decision (complete or incomplete) to move, hinges on two major elements: motives and barriers. They are so important that they need to be investigated in further detail, including the collection and examination of pertinent statistical evidence. To begin with, motives for inter-regional labour migration must be scrutinised more closely.

> It has to be realised, however, that there is yet no such thing as a well-defined concept of motive. The word is here taken as meaning any class of responses to direct or indirect questions on buying reasons, product or brand associations, attitudes, etc. (one can add: reasons for inter-regional labour migration) whose occurrence or non-occurrence on the ground of previous research findings, theoretically founded conclusions, or intuitive insights is believed to influence the number of buyers of a certain product or brand (the number of migrants from one region to another) in the population. The only further condition asked for is that the questions are worded in such a way that buyers (movers) and non-buyers (non-movers) have equal possibilities (though not necessarily equal probabilities) to give the same responses.[9]

But the assessment of motives is not merely a matter of simply asking 'why'. There are reasons for changing, for instance abandoning an old job and residence (complaints or pushes); and there are reasons for choosing among alternative new jobs and residences (specifications, and attractions or pulls).

Research has shown that pushes and pulls are not necessarily identical.[10] Information about migration motives is even more valuable when the reasons cited by respondents are not only measured in terms of frequency, but are also weighted. Where several motives are mentioned it is possible to assess those (or the one) which had the greatest impact on the decision to move. Such impact analysis can be applied to both pushes and pulls—and also to information channels, and thereby, in principle, to all kinds of barriers.[11] Another way of 'weighting' motives is to analyse the interaction of several motives. Basically the procedure consists of assessing how the movers' fraction in the population changes when motives are added to one another and combined in alternative ways.[12] Impact analysis can serve as a form of pre-selection of motives, which are then subject to 'interaction analysis'. Further refinement is achieved by comparing verbal intentions with actual mobility behaviour. This requires the use of panel research.[13]

Some criteria emerge from these considerations for the evaluation of results derived from motivation research:

1. Respondents should represent the whole population, not merely the movers, otherwise there is no control group.

2. It is useful to classify motives into pushes and pulls.

3. These motives, both pushes and pulls, should be weighted by means of impact and interaction-analysis.

4. The importance of the motives should be checked against actual mobility behaviour. This can be done by making predictions on the basis of the motives thought to explain migration, and by comparing the predictions with the results of a follow-up study.

No studies yet fulfil all these 'ideal' requirements. But certain selected research work is in accordance with at least some of these criteria. Only the more important factors which emerge from the statistics are touched upon here. Further details are available, of course, in the studies themselves. Attention has been concentrated on more recent studies in some of the countries covered by this text, France, Great Britain, Sweden; no comparable migration surveys are available for the Netherlands. In some instances we also draw upon specially qualified and outstanding information from such other countries as the United States and Canada.

The reasons most frequently cited for inter-regional movements are economic ones. This can be seen in both national surveys (of Great Britain, Sweden, and the United States[14] and from regional or local case studies (Paris, Göteborg, for instance).[15]

These two case studies, however, do not deal with deviant or extreme phenomena, being rather representative of the countries in question, as a whole. Immigration from all provinces into the Paris region has, and continues, to constitute the bulk of French inter-regional migration (and regional problems), while Göteborg is one of the major receiving areas in Sweden.

Another useful generalisation is that motives vary with the distances moved. The British and Swedish national surveys indicate that the greater the distance, the higher the frequency of job reasons. This corroborates Olsson's suggestion 'that the relevance of the economic factors in migration could be a function of distance'.[16] It has been earlier demonstrated 'that emigration and long distance moves were more strongly related to economic variables than were the short distance ones'.[17]

This implies that the best chance to tap inter-regional, as opposed to other forms of geographical labour migration, exists where the selected regions cover a sufficient number of long distance moves or at least more long than short distance moves. It should be remembered, however, that 'long' and 'short' cannot be defined universally for different countries—in terms of identical numbers of kilometres for the United States and the Netherlands for instance. Since we are concerned with internal migration only, 'long' and 'short' needs to be defined within the context of the country concerned.

It is in such a context that regional labour sub-market areas can be best demarcated.

### 1.2.3   The barriers specified

Motives for inter-regional labour migration—mainly economic motives as surveys show—are necessary but may not be sufficient to transform individual desires to move into actual mobility behaviour. A desire to move might be blocked by various kinds of barriers, which although they sometimes appear in groups are worth separate consideration.

### Lack of opportunities

Since we are dealing with individuals and households, what is considered to be a job opportunity depends on how a situation at some distance is assessed by the individual. As stated such 'objective' observers as civil servants or politicians may differ from individuals and households in their assessment of an opportunity, or more generally in their evaluation of costs and benefits of inter-regional labour migration—especially when their perspective is the national and/or regional viewpoint.

In order to appraise existing migration policies this point must be examined in further detail. Since the move is regarded as the result of a decision-making process, it must be the individual who 'decides' whether or not it takes place. The criteria applied by individuals to judge alternative jobs and residences are as rational in their own context as national or regional criteria are in theirs. Given the individual's decision about say, the kind of job preferred (the dominant reason for moving), barriers which result from a lack of this kind of job can only be broken down, initially, by regional policy which seeks to develop job opportunities on some scale—and this, of course, does not only imply purely quantitative development.

It can, of course, be argued that individual preference scales should be changed, thereby reconciling individual behaviour to national concepts of costs and benefits. Relevant dynamics of the decision-making process will be considered later. At this juncture individual preferences and concepts should be considered as given, in which case barriers to migration result from the fact that the situations preferred by individuals and households do not exist, or not in sufficient numbers.

### Information barriers

Sometimes potential advantageous situations are not realised simply because their existence is not known. They do not, therefore, influence decisions to move. The possibility that preference scales might be changed once sufficient information about new jobs, housing and other amenities becomes available should be remembered here without being considered in detail. Examining

28

surveys with regard to information barriers, we should keep in mind that the criteria mentioned earlier still hold, i.e. the representativeness and scope of the sample, the weighting of different sources of information mentioned by movers and non-movers and also the follow-up. Although not all research results identify which information is lacking but rather focus on information which played a role in the decision to move, these are just the two sides of the same coin. One can call it either an information barrier, or 'enabling factors for successful transfer' (Abramson). Surveying the results of various studies two major kinds of information channel can be distinguished: the informal and the formal.

Some studies (Göteborg; United States) cover both sorts of information channel. Others (Paris; Sweden: Norrbotten County) investigate only the more informal channels of communication. Among the informal ways of obtaining about new residences are the help of friends and relatives. There may be quite strong associations if the individual has previously lived in the new place. Where there has been a continuous stream of migrants from one region to another this itself is sufficient to establish some personal channels of communication. French inter-regional migration between the Auvergne and Paris affords a clear example of this. Macro-studies of inter-regional migration refer in the aggregate to this phenomenon as migration stock [18] or migration fields. [19] Direct contacts with employers through, for instance, the recruiting activities of firms, either in the area of origin or destination can also be classified as informal sources of information in comparison with such formal sources such as printed information contained in advertisements.

Official information services such as those provided by labour offices could

Table 1.5.

Effectiveness of Various Information Sources in the United States

| Information from: | Percentage of those obtaining information | | |
|---|---|---|---|
| | Considering it useful | useless | Not ascertained whether useful |
| Newspaper advertisements | 62.5 | 25.0 | 12.5($N=26$) |
| Employer representative | 80.0 | 10.0 | 10.0($N=33$) |
| Union | 50.0 | 25.0 | 25.0($N=13$) |
| Special trip | 84.0 | 4.0 | 12.0($N=82$) |
| State employment agency | 25.0 | 75.0 | — ($N=13$) |
| Private employment agency | 60.0 | 20.0 | 20.0($N=16$) |
| Friends or relatives | 87.5 | 6.3 | 6.1($N=105$) |
| Other methods | 75.0 | 8.9 | 16.1($N=39$) |

Source: Based on John. B. Lansing *et al.*, op. cit., p. 140.

also be classified formal, though perhaps too much emphasis should not be placed on the terminological distinction between formal and informal information. More important, however, is which of the various sources are the most efficient in promoting a desirable inter-regional move. Although a method for testing the efficiency of information sources has been outlined and demonstrated in some older studies, only Lansing approaches a reliable efficiency check where he seeks to weight the various sources of information cited by respondents.

These responses confirm the primary importance of personal relationships and personal influence,[20] information sources which have been found significant in decision-making processes other than those connected with migration. It embraces a complex communication process, formal information being filtered by the interpretation of advice-giving opinion leaders.[21] It should also be noted that some national employment agency systems might well be more important in this context than others.

## Capability barriers

Three forms of capability can be usefully distinguished: physical, financial and social. The criteria applicable to studies of motives and information channels apply equally to capability (and capability barrier) data.

## Physical capability

To regard good health as a precondition of movement, or ill health as a migration barrier, is common sense, and as can be seen from United States data relating past mobility to perceived health, accords with the facts.

## Financial capability

This also appears to be an obvious and clear-cut factor. Migration policies which rely principally on financial assistance towards economic migration costs apparently attach primary importance to this particular capability aspect. However, it would seem reasonable to attribute part of this resource barrier to such related factors as position in the life-cycle (age, marital status, number of children) and social stratification (education, occupation, etc.). Since these background variables reflect (as is shown below) the basic social capability to move, measures which attempt to deal with pecuniary deficiencies, treat the symptoms instead of the underlying causes.

## Social capability

The factor-complex termed social capability is concerned with 'mobility' strictly defined: that is not with actual behaviour but with basic attitudes towards moving, with the propensity to move. An inter-regional move implies that an innovation has been adopted by an individual or a household.

30

The major determinant of such an adoption is a basic attitude called innovativeness, which may be defined as 'the degree to which an individual is relatively earlier to adopt new ideas than the other members of his social system'.[22] A concrete expression of innovativeness is whether individuals are 'parochial' or cosmopolitan in their attitude of life, which in this context means in their view of potential residences and job locations. Confirming that urban residents tend to be more cosmopolitan than the rural community, a study of the unemployed in Sweden's Norrbotten County revealed a strong correlation between residents grouped by urban and rural locations and moving propensities.[23] Because direct information about innovativeness attitudes is rather scarce in existing studies on inter-regional labour migration, resort must be had to indirect indicator measurement. Rogers has drawn attention to the fact that innovativeness is related to such background variables as social status.

More material is available about these background variables which could be used as proxy indicators of 'attitudinal mobility'.[24] It can now be regarded as established that the higher the socio-economic status of an individual or household (measured in terms of education, occupation, income), the more mobile he or it will be. A second complex of variables closely related to social capability to move are factors pertaining to position in the life-cycle, marital status, number of children and age. The latter is particularly important: the older one is, the less the propensity to move after a certain age.[25]

A third factor, often mentioned in the same context, the degree of home ownership is normally inversely related to mobility. Although home ownership is to some extent associated with social capability features[26] it should perhaps be classified along with financial capability factors. The authors accept this treatment because conditions in the housing market in the area of origin as well as in the destination area determine largely whether home ownership itself constitutes a barrier to migration.[27]

There is another way of measuring social capability. Apart from attitudes and/or such background variables as socio-economic status and position in the life-cycle, actual (past) mobility behaviour can itself be used as an indicator. The method is simply to count the number of past moves, or ascertaining travel frequency in general on the basis that the more people have moved the more mobile they are. This may sound like a tautology, but research has confirmed that actual (past) mobility behaviour can serve in this fashion as a reliable indicator of a certain social capability to move.

For analytical reasons the various aspects of capability and other barriers are treated separately. Many of these phenomena, however, operate in clusters. Whilst therefore it is important to know in principle how the definitions of opportunities, information and social capability influence each other, there are no ready-made research results automatically available for this purpose so that we can only point out certain inter-relationships. For instance, information might change the perception of opportunities and thus remove a migration barrier provided people are dissatisfied with the present situation and therefore motivated to move and provided that alternatives exist. Informativeness is highly correlated with some of the factors that make for social capability, for example with socio-economic status.

To conclude our survey of barrier to migration we should briefly discuss the effects of social ties (to the existing location) on inter-regional labour migration. Integration in the existing home, the location of the reference group—family, friends and so on—normally impede out-migration. Does this constitute a barrier to migration or is it simply a reason for not moving, a lack of motivation? This is not merely a taxonomic matter. The answer may be very relevant to any attempt to evaluate the efficiency of migration programmes. People might be motivated to move for work reasons, but finally stay put because of the kind of social ties mentioned. A pure economic analysis of the costs and benefits of moving might conclude that these people are sufficiently motivated to move because the move would yield higher economic benefits than costs, and the social ties could be seen only as migration barriers. But once the concept of cost-benefit is broadened to include social costs and benefits, and once the actual mobility of the group in question is noted, it might well be concluded that these individuals are simply not motivated to migrate. Such divergent interpretations will be later discussed in some detail, when existing migration programmes of the four countries are evaluated.

### Occupational mobility

At several points reference has been made to sectors, or more precisely to the inter-relation between sectors and inter-regional labour migration. However, it is more appropriate to think in terms of occupations and their training requirements rather than sectors as such. A change of occupation— occupational mobility—can be related to geographical labour migration in a variety of ways. Unfortunately, relevant evidence, especially in the case of long distance moves, is scarce and only a few sources provide information about these relationships. Inter-regional migration and occupational mobility are in part associated: a change in job location and residence can imply a change of occupation, too. When people are released from declining or stagnating activities (for instance agriculture and mining) but remain in the labour force, a prerequisite of getting a job in another sector is occupational mobility.

In monostructured regions where alternative jobs do not exist, at least not in sufficient numbers, people are impelled to (or attracted by) other regions. Training, or more appropriately retraining, may be provided by the new firm or a training centre, but it is possible that the retraining may not be oriented towards a specific job. In this case it is a general aid to mobility, general in the sense that it aims to lower capability barriers to inter-regional migration. Improved occupational status, gained through training for jobs with good prospects or in expanding sectors, enhances the social capability to move. It is not surprising that a low age is more easily associated with occupational mobility than old age, supporting our assertion that both occupational status and position in the life-cycle contribute to general mobility-mindedness or, to use a sociological term, innovativeness. Occupational mobility, especially the retraining process, also influences a second kind of barrier, namely the information barrier. If training is provided for jobs that are not found in the existing area of residence it implies that trainees are informed about job opportunities elsewhere.

When the possibility of occupational mobility is admitted, a new dimension enters the discussion of costs and benefits of bringing jobs to people compared with those of bringing people to jobs. If the jobs brought to the unemployed and new labour force entrants require higher or alternative qualifications, the costs (and benefits) of training (occupational mobility) must be included in the calculation. This holds for the kind of migration policy considered here, where there is a divergence between the qualifications offered and those demanded by jobs in the new area. Provided that alternative jobs are available in the existing location, one could dispense with both efforts to promote labour and capital migration. Measures could concentrate on promoting occupational mobility. As with bringing jobs to people, this could avoid many social costs that arise from moving when the ties with the old place are strong.

Our consideration of motives and barriers has been essentially descriptive. It would have been preferable to present and evaluate motives and barriers more stringently, by, say, discriminant analysis.[28] Such analysis requires, however, a considerable amount of data about individual behaviour and also, for the purpose of this study, comparable data for four countries. The conditions for an aggregate (regional) analysis of migration were also not ideal, but relatively more favourable, and it was decided to carry out a more rigorous (though less 'behavioural') analysis at the regional level (Section 1.3). Further action-oriented research, however, should ideally start with the decision-making aspects of individual and household migration.

### 1.2.4 Dynamics of the migration process: the follow-up

We have described the process of moving in a somewhat 'static' way: as a process with a clear-cut beginning (dissatisfaction with existing job and residence) and end (an actual move to a new location or action blocked by barriers). However, research has clearly indicated that moving is a process, which continues once a migrant has arrived at a new location. He may consider his move temporary or a trial, or he may fail to adapt to the new situation. In both cases movement continues, sometimes back, sometimes to other places. Only if a migrant adjusts can we consider the case closed, and then only for the time being. In order to identify these various types of migration history it is necessary to extend research (and theory) so that it embraces the aftermath of the decision to move. This implies that research should trace the migrant's history over a period of time, ideally his life-cycle.[29]

But does a special follow-up problem exist? Would it not be sufficient to study a second move (or non-move) in exactly the same way as the first, explaining it in terms of motives and barriers? This would be acceptable, if the first move had no immediate impact on a potential return, but experience shows that adjustment to a new location is uncertain, so that the likelihood of moving back or elsewhere grows with the uncertainty of becoming adjusted.

It follows that studying the aftermath means shifting the emphasis from motives (i.e. initial dissatisfaction) and barriers to the process of becoming dissatisfied (or satisfied) and thus motivated (or unmotivated) to move. Barriers are very much the same if retirement moves are left out of account and if we focus attention on members still in the labour force. What does research tell us about the reasons for dissatisfaction with, and a failure to integrate into, a new residence and job location? There is little relevant research evidence available. It is much easier to undertake another migration study than to try to cover the follow-up by means of panel research.

Among the studies concerned with the follow-up process two are especially informative, the Göteborg study and a Canadian study that provides a preliminary prediction model for successful (or otherwise) integration. Research results suggest that there are two basically different groups of incoming migrants. First there are those who do not intend to settle down, who make a 'trial move' and sometimes have made plans to move even before they arrive. Once this group is identified, it is not surprising to find its members among those returning home or moving on. Secondly there are those who try to settle down but for various reasons fail to do so. The reasons might be termed 'barriers to integration' and it should be noted, refer to those areas where barriers to migration are usually found.

Absence of a job opportunity due, for instance, to a recession, may emerge after arrival. More probable, however, is the case where movers overestimate the job attractions of the area, a matter concerned with information. An overestimate of job opportunities is caused by inadequate or imprecise information in the home area. There are forms of disappointment associated with work in the new area: they may stem from the enterprise, or from the kind of job—say assembly line work—which is characteristic of a whole sector.

Another potential source of discontent is housing. Although housing does not rate very highly as a reason for leaving the area (for long distance moves at any rate) it might effectively block a move when people find it difficult to sell their house in their existing area and/or to buy or rent a house in the new one. Whether this happens depends on conditions in the housing market, which can be as misinterpreted as those attached to work, if information is deficient. In fast growing areas with a 'natural' housing shortage it is very probable that integration will be hampered by housing disappointments especially when in-migrants must live in such temporary accommodation as barracks.

There is also a factor akin to capability to adapt. Ill-health and lack of resources—especially among people who were unemployed prior to migration—may induce in-migrants to return or move on. But again, we would like to emphasise a less visible aspect of capability, namely social capability. Parochials—people moving from rural to urban areas, pushed into migration by unemployment and having strong social ties with their origin—have special trouble settling down and establishing new social contacts etc. The background variable of these difficulties is a low propensity to move, or low innovativeness. If it cannot be measured directly low educational levels and low status occupations are proxy indicators of this particular attitude. Their inter-relation with informativeness points to the likelihood of barriers to integration appearing in clusters.

Since job opportunities constitute the most important motive the monetary return to migration may be the best single indicator of migration success. Recently attempts have been made to calculate the 'net return to migration' defined as 'the present value of the increase in the flow of monetary and psychic income less the present value of the flow of monetary and psychic costs resulting from the move'.[30] Any benefit-cost approach to inter-regional, and other types, of labour migration must assess the net return to migration.[31] However empirical measurement is confined, as in the case of the Wertheimer and Jenness studies, to the monetary dimension of migration success, no satisfactory measurement has yet been devised. The Göteborg study, again, illustrates the wage and other dimensions (housing, social contacts) of migration success, testifying to the fact-finding potential of follow-up studies even if they cover a period of only 6–7 months after the initial move.

A theoretically promising avenue has been opened by Jane Abramson.[32] After measuring the degree of adjustment of rural migrants to urban life, the success or failure of personal adjustment is explained by a set of factors pertaining to those integration barriers described above. Thus it becomes possible to predict fairly accurately the chances of satisfactory urban adjustment before people move. Although the final judgement about this predictive technique remains to be made, the approach seems to be of great practical importance. If migration policy attempts not only to promote long distance migration, but also to settle people in the new location, predicting the probability of a mover becoming adjusted to the new milieu permits the identification of those who are in need of special 'receiving' aid.

Table 1.6 helps to summarise what has been said about the follow-up of inter-regional labour migration.

Table 1.6.

A Paradigm of the Follow-Up Process in Inter-regional Migration of Labour

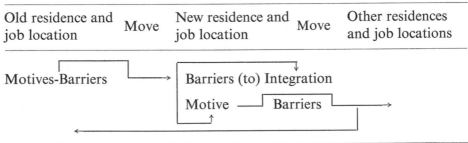

| Old residence and job location | Move | New residence and job location | Move | Other residences and job locations |
|---|---|---|---|---|

Motives-Barriers

Barriers (to) Integration

Motive — Barriers

### 1.2.5   Another dynamic aspect: influencing motives and barriers

In addition to the follow-up there is another dynamic aspect of inter-regional labour movement that is particularly relevant to migration policy: the degree of constancy of motives and barriers. How much time does it take to change motives and barriers, if in the face of attempts to move people to jobs a given constellation of motives and barriers produces, at a given moment, immobility.[33] What national, 'objective', observers consider as hindrances need not necessarily coincide with the views of the individuals and households directly involved. Notions about the costs and benefits of moving vary and one cannot move people who are satisfied with their existing residence and job and hence who are not motivated to move. The appreciation of opportunities might be changed once improved information about new residences and jobs is available and also with better education (which already implies institutional changes). But there remains the question of the pushes which need to be 'produced'. Negative measures do not figure among the usual instruments of migration policy. Better information and education can only produce dissatisfaction or relative deprivation through higher aspiration levels. This may be only a long-term effect so that trying to mobilise the unmotivated[34] may yield poor results in the short run.

Matters are different when one looks at those who are motivated, but blocked by barriers in their decision.[35] Typical barriers which can usually be removed in the short run are information and financial barriers although the implementation of the respective programmes may take time. Indeed where there is no established and efficient network of say labour offices, the time required may stretch into the long term.

The lack of job opportunities and the presence of social capability barriers are typically long-term phenomena. In order to overcome the former on a significant scale an effective regional policy, developing the required job opportunities, is needed. This process might sometimes be shortened by selective programmes of job creation of the sort provided in the American demonstration projects,[36] although this is not always successful on a large scale which requires more time. Social capability, and its key determinant education or training is in a comparable position. If social capability barriers exist on a large (regional) scale they can probably be removed only by broad educational programmes—usually implying institutional changes. Certain retraining devices, however, might shorten the time required, especially for selected groups. A particularly difficult situation occurs when inadequate education and old age are associated. To the time normally needed to train or retrain young people must be added the time required to break down a double capability barrier, resulting from inadequate education and old age. In these situations such alternative measures as redundancy payments or early pensions must be considered, since lowering the barriers for this hard-core group consumes too much time and money.

Our statements about the treatment of motives and barriers must necessarily be tentative in nature, given the paucity of research evidence. In a policy-oriented book, however, the subject should at least be touched upon and a plea entered that the field should be further explored. The latter suggestion reinforces the demand for more follow-up studies (panel research) —ideally studies of migration histories.

## 1.3 An aggregate view of inter-regional labour migration in France, Great Britain, the Netherlands and Sweden

So far we have regarded inter-regional labour migration as a decision-making process at the individual and household level. This view afforded insight into the factors making for moves or non-moves, namely certain constellations of motives and barriers. Such an approach is especially suitable for consulting individuals and households in order to ensure the desired mobility behaviour. However politicians, concerned with migration usually base their attitudes on aggregate inter-regional labour migrations. After examining actual volume and direction of migration flows and considering the structures of the regions involved, national policy-makers may decide either to encourage development along its existing course or to reverse its general direction. Factors normally taken into account when formulating migration policy are the existence of pockets of regional unemployment and labour shortages; regional income differentials and diseconomies of scale in large metropolitan areas, etc. Net migration often serves as the indicator for designating desired origins and destinations ('losers' or 'winners') for inter-regional labour migration. The identification of 'losers', especially on the basis of negative regional net migration, induces the authorities to influence geographical labour migration.

Therefore the main reason why inter-regional labour migration should also be considered in the aggregate, is essentially political. And a policy paper cannot avoid these political realities simply by establishing arbitrary, if convenient, boundaries of competences. There can be no doubt that migration policy is inextricably intertwined with regional policy whether the latter is narrowly defined as regional industrialisation or as policies for the socio-economic development of urban and rural areas. When presenting an aggregate picture of inter-regional labour migration in France, Great Britain, the Netherlands and Sweden, however, two problems emerge:

1. What is the appropriate level of regional aggregation, and what are 'meaningful' regions at this level in the countries under consideration?

2. How can the magnitude of migration be ascertained, in terms of net migration or of directional flows?

### 1.3.1 The demarcation of regions

What regions in the four countries are meaningful in the context of government action to influence inter-regional labour migration? Before answering this question for each country we think it is useful to determine the more essential demarcation criteria.

1. It has been said that (physical) distance plays a decisive role in distinguishing inter-regional migration from other forms of geographical labour migration, because there is evidence that the greater the distance moved, the higher the frequency of work reasons. This means that the regions most be chosen in a way that ensures the movers cover sufficiently long distances in order to catch inter-regional labour migration of the kind which concerns us here. It has also been said that there is no universal yardstick for delimiting long and short distances. This must be decided within the context of the country in question, otherwise extremely misleading results might emerge. Using American dimensions a country

such as the Netherlands would be reduced to a single region or, at best, two.

2. The regions should have a politico-administrative relevance. This means that either regional policy systems should apply for the achievement of more or less autonomous regional goals, and/or that national policies and goals should be regionalised.

3. Usually, however, politico-administrative units represent the levels at which migration statistics are compiled. This is very practical, because only a numerical record of moves renders inter-regional labour movements susceptible to theoretical analysis, to explanation and prediction. And such theoretical analysis provides the basis for a rational migration policy, instead of one built on trial and error.

## France

For France we have chosen the twenty-one *régions de programme*, constituted by the administrative reform of 1964. These regions represent combinations of the ninety-five *départements* hence improving the likelihood of measuring real inter-regional migration. Of course short distance moves cannot be completely excluded, especially in the case of metropolitan areas such as the Paris region with its spread of dwellings and jobs into the surrounding regions of Picardie, Haute-Normandie, and Centre. The aggregation simply enables us to get 'more' long distance moves by choosing programme regions rather than counties (*départements*) but as far as the politico-administrative criterion is concerned, it is not certain that it is served by our preference for regions instead of counties. Regional levels have not developed, but have been implanted by law,[37] and have been the subject of discussion ever since. In any case official planning in France, including migration policy, is concerned with programme regions.[38] In the period, 1960–8, in which we are interested, policies dealt with programme regions and we are obliged to do the same.

Finally, there is the criterion of data availability. Migration data (from censuses) are available both at the county and regional levels, implying various ways of data analysis at the regional level. Thus, for the purpose of this policy-oriented book, it was decided to regard France's twenty-one *régions de programme* as labour market areas, that is the regional sub-markets of the French labour market.

## Great Britain

For Great Britain the designated economic planning regions have been chosen. Some problems are caused by a change in the number of regions in 1965 when the former standard regions were replaced by the revised standard regions which correspond (except in one instance) to the economic planning regions. In order to make post-1965 data comparable with earlier data the regional units have to be reconciled, reducing the number to eight[39]. On the one hand, the South East and East Anglia and, on the other, the East Midlands and Yorkshire and Humberside are combined in order to match former standard regions.

Do these units fulfil our criteria? Without a further reduction in the number of regions, this seems the best possible way of covering a great number of long distance moves. It is unavoidable, hovever, that some of the old standard regions (and economic planning regions) to some extent cut across the boundaries of city regions and commuting zones. The economic planning regions constitute the geographical units with which regional planning in Britain is concerned. Since they were established recently, in 1964 and 1965, the question posed in the case of France is also pertinent here. Are these economic planning regions political and administrative realities? More precisely, it must be inquired whether the planning machinery at the newly regional level is sufficient operational and sufficient organised to make the regions practically relevant. To answer this question is beyond the scope of created regional level is sufficiently operational and efficient to make these this study.[40] Therefore we adhere to the official blueprint for regions, leaving us with eight 'labour market areas' for Great Britain.

## The Netherlands

The eleven provinces of the Netherlands are adopted as the regional units. Distances in 'universal' kilometres are already very 'short'—the maximum distance is between Middelburg, centre of the South-Western province of Zeeland, and Groningen in the North, namely 361 auto-kilometres.

Thus focusing attention on inter-provincial streams appears to be the only feasible way of catching long distance moves, that is moves which are 'long' in the Dutch context. Serious reservations arise primarily in the case of the Dutch Rimcity, touching the three provinces of Zuid-Holland, Noord-Holland (a large part of it) and Utrecht, where parts of suburban and intra-regional migration are unavoidably treated as inter-regional—and the Rimcity is rapidly expanding into adjacent parts of Gelderland and Noord-Brabant. Although the Rimcity as a whole may well constitute a local labour market, this remains to be demonstrated and the provincial boundaries are, at present, most relevant since real Rimcity planning does not yet exist. The Dutch planning concept as expressed in the *Tweede Nota*,[41] special regional programmes and actual planning practice, testifies to the relevance of provinces in a politico-administrative sense. Also migration data are available at the provincial level, so that they can serve as regional labour markets.

*Sweden*

For Sweden twenty-three counties (*länen*) have been chosen as regional [42] units. Such a demarcation appears to screen a sufficient number of long distance moves without, however, completely avoiding the problem that arises in metropolitan areas. Stockholm city and county were amalgamated in 1968.

No separate analysis of, on the one hand, local labour market impacts on migration and, on the other, pure residential migration (suburbanisation) can be carried out. Perhaps this is not so important a qualification in Sweden as in France (with the Paris region), Great Britain (Greater London) and the Netherlands (the Dutch Rimcity) because it is not yet as highly metropolised as these countries. This might be a later phase in Sweden's process of urbanisation. Even with the country's high degree of centralisation the counties have sufficient politico-administrative relevance. It clearly makes sense to categorise the Norrbotten area as one of unemployment and the Göteborg area as one of labour shortage. Thus the counties seem to constitute meaningful labour market areas, data about which is documented in migration statistics.

### 1.3.2 Directional flows and net migration

There are two basic methods of ascertaining the magnitude of inter-regional migration in our countries: assessing 'magnitude' in terms of directional flows and 'magnitude' in terms of net migration. Directional flows have been adopted on the following grounds:

1. No individual can be classified as a 'net migrant'; there are simply in- or out-migrants. If we consider directional flows and net migration at the regional level it is even possible to identify different determinants, especially when such relevant economic indicators as unemployment (vacancies) and/or income differentials are introduced.[43] Such factors may well explain why *more* people are leaving (arriving) than arriving (leaving), while there are still people moving into areas with unemployment (negative income differentials) or leaving regions with vacancies (positive income differentials). Directional flows thus approximate more closely the individual or household decision-making, while net migration constitutes a regional property for which one settles if one is solely interested in whether more people are leaving than arriving, or vice versa.

2. A more disaggregated view about the magnitude of inter-regional labour migration is needed than that provided by net-migration, because 'behind a given net migration sum *any* gross migration figure could be hidden' (Andersson and Jungen).

41

Both the volume of in- and out-migration, measuring the turnover of members of the labour force and their dependents is indeed important to migration politicians given their concern for the 'turnover' of jobs, houses, amenities, etc. But even more than the total figure it is important to obtain information about the composition of the incoming (outgoing) streams of migrants, especially about their age and skill characteristics. Regions with zero net migration in quantitative terms may nevertheless be gainers or losers in qualitative terms. Positive and negative net migration may also be devalued or 'revalued' when the quality of in- and out-migration is investigated. Such an investigation, however, is often hampered by a lack of relevant disaggregation in in- and out-migration flows. An illustration of the value of breakdowns of inter-regional migration is afforded by French census data about the socio-occupational structure.[44] Once qualitative breakdowns of directional migration flows are available, it is not difficult to compute more aggregated indicators such as net migration by social occupation.

Considerations like these underline the importance of placing inter-regional labour migration in the context of *national* and *regional labour markets* or *manpower balances*. Hence both statistical indicators (directional flows and net migration, qualities and quantities) and theoretical approaches can be judged upon their contribution to the description, explanation, prediction and control of the nation's regional sub-labour markets. Especially in the case of net migration, theoretical interpretations can vary widely. While some observers believe that differential rates of migration are induced by differential changes in job opportunities or employment,[45] others regard differential changes in employment as induced by differential rates of in-migration.[46] Muth found statistical evidence supporting the hypothesis that migration and employment growth each affect and are affected by the other.[47] And there are even more comprehensive labour market models which incorporate migration.[48]

3. An additional disadvantage of net migration indicators is the fact that usually they do not distinguish migrants by type of geographical labour migration. This can be cumbersome if one wishes to exclude from the analysis as much pure residential migration (for instance suburbanisation) as possible. A first stage demarcation, however, can be achieved when choosing the regional level at which net migration is reported. As stated, this level of aggregation must be appropriate in the context of the country being studied.[49] 'Exclusiveness' with regard to purely residential moves can be checked by introducing distances as independent variables and testing their impact on net migration. This of course requires that, for instance, net migration is calculated on the basis of directional flows for

pairs of regions—not the usual procedure and one which presupposes knowledge of directional flows.

4. There is also a very practical reason for preferencing directional flows to net migration. Net migration is usually small in comparison with flows and may therefore largely reflect measurement errors. This is so in Great Britain where users of the 1966 sample census are warned about the presence of appreciable bias, under-enumeration and serious errors in the five-year migration data—apart from the normal sample error. Thus an analysis of net migration data may sometimes be concerned essentially with a statistical artifact.

To conclude this section we would like to point out that net migration, especially if it is negative, functions as a form of alarm. But every region wants to be a winner, so that plans are rarely made on the assumption of a further decrease in population growth. Nevertheless, the regions do face a zero-sum problem, and (assuming that foreign in- and out-migration is to be balanced) if one region is to be a winner others must be losers. Appropriate analysis, especially at the national level for all the regional sub-markets usually introduces 'zero-sum consistency' into planning. The question then arises whether an aggregate analysis of inter-regional labour migration should be carried out in terms of directional flows and/or net migration. Reasons for preferring directional flows in a study such as this have been set out above. Net migration is therefore regarded as a second best solution. Sometimes, however, it is the only statistically feasible solution, in which case its limitations should be known. Directional flows, hopefully broken down by qualitative features, not only provide a better insight into a region's development problems but probably also a superior basis for prescribing remedies.

### 1.3.3  Statistical data

It would be unrealistic to hope for a completely comparable analysis for all four countries. For one thing, such an attempt would be prevented by the usual differences in statistical reportage, and by the definition of regions within each country. Within these limits, however, we will try to make the analysis as comparable as possible. Since the demarcation of regions has been discussed, it is appropriate to start with a description of the statistical sources used in our analysis.

In France there was no statistical choice. To survey migration streams in the sixties, it was necessary to adhere to 1968 census data. In that year a population sample was asked where they lived in 1962. Thus this source provided information about the number of individuals surviving in 1968

43

from inter-regional migration between 1962 and 1968. Actual inter-regional migration during that period is underestimated for three reasons:

1. Not all the movements of people during 1962–8 are registered, only their last ones.

2. The moves of those who died or left the country in the period, also fail to be recorded.

3. And the same is true for return movers.

But since, as already stated, there was no alternative source, we possess only an 'underestimate' of French inter-regional labour migration for a period of six successive years.

We found a somewhat better statistical situation in Great Britain, but only because there is more choice. The 'census survival approach' adopted in Britain yields data for both one-year movers (1966/65 and 1961/60) and five-year movers (1966/61). The latter have been chosen since they approximate more closely the French concepts. In the census year 1966, people were asked where they had lived in April 1961. Once again the true volume of migration is underestimated to an unknown extent.

Fig. 1.1.   Periods for which Inter-regional Labour Migration will be studied in the Four Countries.

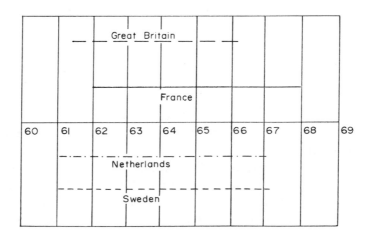

The Netherlands statistical reportage presents few problems. At the time when this analysis was carried out the most recent data available were for 1966. Thus one year (1967) is cut off in comparison with France, but on the other hand there is a closer approximation to Britain's five year data, both at the end and the beginning of the period.

It is not difficult to adapt the relevant Swedish data to the Dutch data, since both countries use the event-reporting method. It is necessary only to have to dispense with Swedish data for 1967 in order to achieve comparability with the Netherlands in terms of observation periods.

Thus we have at our disposal, two sets of census data and two sets of full annual information about inter-regional migration.[50] The regions are defined pragmatically within the context of each country. In Figure 1.1 the time periods covered by the available migration data are compared for each country. The complete picture of inter-regional labour migration in France, Great Britain, the Netherlands and Sweden is shown by origin-destination matrices.[51]

### 1.3.4 A parsimonious model of inter-regional migration

Our aggregate approach has been directed towards the directional flows of migration. The next step is to explain the volume and direction of these flows in our four countries. It is beyond the scope of this book to trace in detail the history of macro-models of inter-regional migration; there has emerged only one basic framework involving several variations of deterministic or probabilistic types of model. Deterministic models yielded satisfactory results for us, so that a probabilistic alternative was not considered. In consequence the model used does not differ radically from earlier aggregate models, either in its logical structure or in the selection of explanatory factors.[52] Our own model might be termed a parsimonious labour market model in that it views migration as a reaction of units of labour supply in one region to units of labour demand in other regions, in relation to migration costs (interpreted in a wide sense). Ideally, this view of regional sub-markets requires considerable disaggregation, especially in connection with the quality dimension of labour demand and supply—as in the case of France where relevant data are provided by the breakdown by socio-occupational groups. Further research into this aspect—and also into alternative approaches of the probabilistic type[53] and more comprehensive regional models[54]—is both *needed* and *practicable*.[55]

Our hypothesis for the determinants of inter-regional migration is as follows. The magnitude of migration flow from region $i$ to region $j$ is directly related to the total number of non-agricultural jobs in $j$ (destination) and to the total labour force in $i$ (origin), and is inversely proportional to the distance between origin and destination. Thus the larger the number of non-agricultural jobs in $j$, the larger the labour force in $i$, and the shorter the distance between $i$ and $j$, the greater will be the number of migrants moving from $i$ to $j$.

In algebraic terms we have:

$$_{12}M_{ij} = \alpha_0 \frac{_0E_j^{\alpha_1} \cdot {_0}L_i^{\alpha_2}}{_{10}\alpha_3 D_{ij}}$$

where

$_{12}M_{ij} =$ total number of migrants from region $i$ to region $j$ (during period 12)

$_0E_j \quad =$ total number of non-agricultural jobs (industry and services) in region $j$ (in the base year 0)

$_0L_i \quad =$ total number of people 15 to 65 years of age (labour force) in region $i$ (also in year 0)

$D_{ij} \quad =$ distance between the centres of region $i$ and $j$ in auto-kilometres.

According to the mathematical form of the equation, it is assumed that the aggregate regional supply of and demand for labour in, say, 1960, stimulates migration throughout a number of subsequent years (e.g. 1961–6). The explanatory variables introduced merit further comment. The number of non-agricultural jobs[56] is regarded as the aggregate expression of the factor most frequently cited at the individual and household level, for undertaking long-distance, inter-regional migration: job opportunities. It might be argued that the number of vacancies would be a better indicator but there are some doubts about this because information concerning vacancies is usually derived from employment agencies and such information (the same is true of unemployment data) tends to refer only to marginal groups in the labour market. What is really required is a disaggregation of regional demand for labour, as it is measured here, by level of skill required. Since this must be left to future research, we prefer to use the crude aggregate, bearing its deficiencies in mind.

Counting jobs in the secondary and tertiary sectors means counting 'objective' or 'actual' job opportunities. Whether or not they correspond to a mover's definition, to 'apparent' opportunities, can be tested. If the regression coefficient $\alpha_1$ proves to be statistically significant, then our hypothesis that inter-regional migration is mainly job-oriented is not contradicted and our regional demarcations can be regarded as covering a satisfactory amount of labour migration.

The regional labour force is represented by the number of people between 15 and 65 years of age.[57] This seems the least ambiguous definition, and one which ensures a high degree of comparability. It is of course only a crude estimate, since not all people in this age bracket are economically active: participation rates are sometimes remarkably different between countries, especially for women (for instance, Sweden and the Netherlands). A degree of disaggregation—say by skill level—is again desirable and possible, though not at this juncture. For the time being we use $_0L_i$ to represent a typical potential variable, the potential regional labour supply, and the degree to which this potential is activated by job stimuli and hampered by distance (manifesting itself in $n$ moves) is measured by $\alpha_2$. We might have used 'pushes' as expressed, for instance, by unemployment rates. However, as stated, registered unemployment rates only refer to marginal elements in the labour force, and in any case a potential mover may seek a better position without being unemployed. Unless the labour force is disaggregated by skill level, the use of the potential variable and an average rate of 'mobilisation' $\alpha_2$ seems preferable.

Distance between regional centres is measured in auto-kilometres[58]. These centres have been determined rather pragmatically: most of them being politico-administrative centres or 'regional capitals' but sometimes gravity centres have been used. There are alternative approaches, but the major interest centres around the question of what physical distance means in theoretical terms. Some research has already been carried out on this topic and new analyses of this key variable of inter-regional labour migration suggest themselves.[59]

An important result is the discovery of evidence for informational (communicational) distance. The negative relationship between migration flow and physical distance can be transformed into a positive relationship between flow and existing information (communication channels). If physical distance $(D_{ij})$ is introduced its regression coefficient $(\alpha_3)$ no doubt measures both 'economic' and 'non-economic' elements. Traditionally, economic elements are the direct migration costs, namely transportation costs and such indirect costs as opportunity costs. Should a migrant from region $i$ to region $j$ traverse regions with attractive job opportunities, the number of intervening opportunities[60] tends to reduce the number of migrants from $i$ to $j$. Among 'non-economic' elements are the 'costs associated with moving away from one's family and friends' (Greenwood) or from a 'known' to an 'unknown' milieu. These costs are less if there are friends and relatives in the new location. Costs are higher the more pronounced the differences in culture, social structure, etc. between the new and old locations. If the regions of a country covered by our analysis are identified with distinct social cultures[61] then inter-regional physical distances most probably reflect a good deal of 'social distance' (which, however, can always be mitigated by 'migration fields', 'migration stocks' and the like).

## 1.3.5 Results

The short cut appraisal of regional labour markets, as implied by our parsimonious migration model, has been tested for the four countries.[62] The major statistical results are presented in Table 1.7, a table which reveals the extent to which a simple labour market model can explain the magnitude of directional flows of inter-regional labour migration.

If it is agreed that mobility should be measured by all the regression coefficients, including the intercept, then a clear rank order—say one country higher (or lower) on all positive (or negative) coefficients, another country second, another third and the last one fourth—can be interpreted as a rank

Table 1.7.

Regression Statistics: Data for France (F), Great Britain (GB), Netherlands (NL) and Sweden (S), 1960–8[1]

| Variable | | Intercept, regression and multiple correlation coefficient | Standard error of regression coefficient and of estimate | Partial correlation coefficient |
|---|---|---|---|---|
| $\log \alpha_0$ | F | −4.93810 | | |
| | GB | −4.53010 | | |
| | NL | −1.46200 | | |
| | S | −2.96300 | | |
| $\log E_j$ | F | .99713* | .04930 | .51241 |
| | GB | .85790* | .09783 | .53955 |
| | NL | .58690* | .04340 | .52543 |
| | S | .82949* | .04873 | .38600 |
| $\log L_i$ | F | 1.06450* | .05700 | .45828 |
| | GB | .93334* | .11047 | .50250 |
| | NL | .61246* | .04863 | .49789 |
| | S | .76954* | .05627 | .50106 |
| $D_{ij}$ | F | − .00100* | .00006 | −.38870 |
| | GB | − .00095* | .00018 | −.40399 |
| | NL | − .00409* | .00019 | −.83933 |
| | S | − .00062* | .00004 | −.53182 |
| R | F | .83030† | .28174 | |
| | GB | .87207* | .20252 | |
| | NL | .95943* | .15021 | |
| | S | .78945† | .27773 | |

[1] See Figure 1.1.
* Significantly different from zero at a level of confidence < .001
† Significantly different from zero at .05 level of confidence.

order of inter-regional mobility of the French, English, Dutch and Swedish. Mobility measured in this way would be relative to the factors introduced, primarily to the regional supply of and demand for labour—which in turn are influenced by the regional demarcations. The result might be referred to as the propensity to move for work reasons. The higher $\alpha_1$ and $\alpha_2$ the more mobile would be the populations of the countries studied in this respect. As distance is shown to reduce the volume of inter-regional migration, the lower is $\alpha_3$, the more mobile is the population. An overall comparison of mobility could only be made on the basis of the size of the weighted complex of all coefficients.

This principle is demonstrated in Table 1.8. The method consists of introducing equal standardised values for the variables in each equation, followed by a comparison of the resulting migration flows. It is thus a comparison of the flows that would result in each of the four countries if conditions in those countries as far as distance, job opportunities and potential working force were identical. First, the results of the regression analysis are repeated. (For complete results see Table 1.7.)

Table 1.8.

Results of Regression Analysis

| Country | $\log \alpha_0$ | $\alpha_1$ | $\alpha_2$ | $\alpha_3$ |
|---|---|---|---|---|
| France | −4.94 | 0.997 | 1.065 | −0.00100 |
| Great Britain | −4.53 | 0.858 | 0.933 | −0.00095 |
| Sweden | −2.96 | 0.829 | 0.770 | −0.00062 |
| Netherlands | −1.46 | 0.587 | 0.612 | −0.00409 |

There is a clear-cut, but reverse, rank order in the coefficients $\log \alpha_0$ on the one hand and $\alpha_2$ on the other. Higher values of $\log \alpha_0$ (smaller negative values of $\log \alpha_0$) are found in countries where the values of $\alpha_1$ and $\alpha_2$ are low. This rank order tends to be found in the distance coefficient excepting the Netherlands where the influence of distance is large compared with that in other countries. Thus the conflicting patterns of these coefficients make it impossible to present a definitive ranking of mobility in the four countries. In order to obtain such a result we adopt the procedure described above. First the equations for four distances, 50, 100, 200 and 300 km are given in Table 1.9.

In this table, $\pi$ represents $\log L_i E_j$. Coefficients $\alpha_1$ and $\alpha_2$ have been averaged out over $L_i$ and $E_j$. It would seem that the ranking order of the con-

Table 1.9.

Value of $\log M_{ij}$ for Four Distances

| $D_{ij}$ | F | GB | S | NL |
|---|---|---|---|---|
| 50 | $-4.99+\pi$ | $-4.58+0.9\pi$ | $-2.99+0.8\pi$ | $-1.66+0.6\pi$ |
| 100 | $-5.04+\pi$ | $-4.63+0.9\pi$ | $-3.02+0.8\pi$ | $-1.86+0.6\pi$ |
| 200 | $-5.14+\pi$ | $-4.72+0.9\pi$ | $-3.08+0.8\pi$ | $-2.28+0.6\pi$ |
| 300 | $-5.24+\pi$ | $-4.82+0.9\pi$ | $-3.15+0.8\pi$ | $-2.69+0.6\pi$ |

stants does not alter with rising distances, although the relative position of the Netherlands changes more rapidly than that of the other countries.

The next stage is to compare the migration volume over two distances (100 km and 300 km) for different levels of job opportunities. This is carried out in Graphs 1.1 and 1.2, the former being constructed for $D_{ij}=100$ km and the latter for $D_{ij}=300$ km. It appears that, under *identical* conditions in terms of the relevant variables, total migration in Holland is largest of all the four countries for all values of $\pi<6$, which means for migration flows between regions up to an average value of one million for both $L_i$ and $E_j$. For $D_{ij}=300$, the Dutch are still the most mobile for smaller values of $\log L_i E_j$ (smaller regions), but for larger values the Swedish emerge as the most mobile.

Another way of analysing these results, is to compare migration flows induced by raising $E_j$, that is by increasing the number of job opportunities in $j$.[63] To a certain extent this represents the evaluation of a regional policy to raise the number of job opportunities. In Table 1.10 the results are presented for two pairs of the relevant variables, that is for $D_{ij}$ equal to 100 and 300 km respectively, and for $L_i E_j$ equal to $100,000^2$ and $1,000,000^2$.

Table 1.10.

Additional Number of Migrants from $i$ Induced by the Creation of 1000 Jobs in $j$

| $D_{ij}$ | Between 'small' regions | | Between 'large' regions | |
|---|---|---|---|---|
| | 100 | 300 | 100 | 300 |
| NL | 25.0 | 3.9 | 49.0 | 6.2 |
| S | 12.0 | 9.0 | 42.0 | 36.0 |
| GB | 0.8 | 0.8 | 5.3 | 3.4 |
| F | 0.6 | 0.5 | 9.3 | 5.6 |

Graph 1.1.    Levels of log $M_{ij}$ for different values of log $L_i E_j$

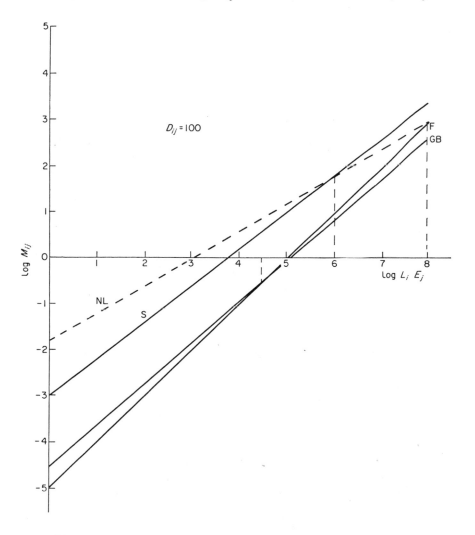

## Graph 1.2. Levels of log $M_{ij}$ for different levels of log $L_i E_j$

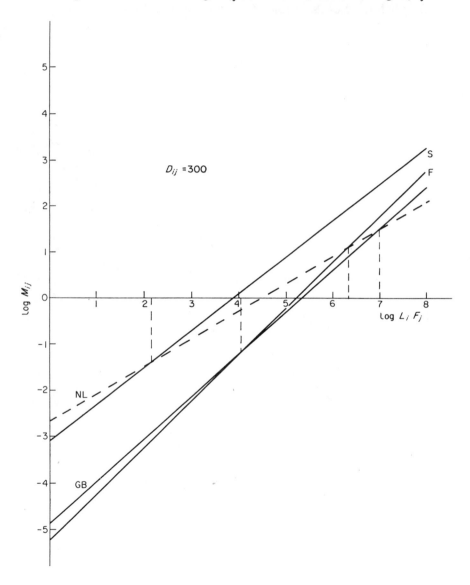

We will call the regions for which $L_iE_j$ is $100,000^2$, small regions, and those where $L_iE_j$ is $1,000,000^2$, large, although $L_iE_j=100,000^2$ could result from a value for $L_i$ of 10,000, and for $E_j$ of 1,000,000.

The following conclusions might be drawn from these results. First, the effectiveness of job creation in terms of induced migration is largest in the Netherlands and Sweden, especially between small regions and between large regions for smaller distances. The effectiveness of job creation is extremely low in Great Britain and France. Secondly, the effectiveness of job creation in the Netherlands decreases very rapidly with distance. With a distance of 300 km its effectiveness in the Netherlands is as low as in France and not very much different from that in Great Britain. Sweden has a very high rank as far as the results for long distances are concerned. A general conclusion might be that mobility is highest in the Netherlands for smaller distances and in Sweden for larger distances. It is least in Great Britain and France. It is interesting to try to 'explain' the differences in the four countries' distance coefficients. It seems reasonable to assume that the country's size is one relevant factor.

Graph 1.3 presents the relationship between the distance influence and average regional distance. The smallest country, Holland (where the mean inter-regional distance is 173 km, displays the highest distance-sensitivity of inter-regional movers. As we saw earlier, this may well imply low labour mobility with respect to long distance moves, though not a low overall labour mobility.

At the other extreme is Sweden, with the longest average inter-regional distance, 490 km, and the lowest distance-sensitivity. Of course, scope for the substitution of commuting for inter-regional mobility, is limited in such a big country as Sweden. But still there remains an intriguing question: why, in Sweden, should physical distance matter little. On average, distance, measured in terms of number of migrants which moved the same (long) distance and thereby created communication channels, may be shorter than physical distance. This leads back to Hägerstrand and his migration fields, an idea which perhaps significantly was developed to help explain migration in Sweden. It would seem that regional labour supplies and demands do not respond to each other as easily as they do in other countries, but migration fields appear to make people relatively less distance-sensitive, other things being equal, once they have decided to move. This interpretation, however, is tentative.

Other questions arise from Graph 1.3. Distances mean more for the French than for Swedish movers, although on average distances they are nearly the same, 487 compared with 490 km. On the basis of the hypothesis advanced for the Swedish case, social distance relative to physical distance should on average be higher in France in comparison with Sweden. Whether

Graph 1.3.   Distance influence and country 'size' in France, Great Britain, The Netherlands and Sweden.

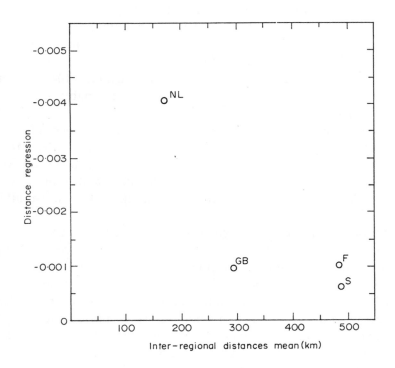

differences in urbanisation between regions are greater in France than in Sweden, and whether this implies greater social distances because inter-regional migration involves a change of radically different social milieus and life-styles, cannot be determined from these results. Another interesting fact to emerge is that even countries with contrasts in average inter-regional distance, namely Great Britain (295 km) and France (487 km), display roughly the same degree of distance-sensitivity. The commuting effect may explain at least part of the relatively high distance-elasticity in Great Britain, and physical and social distances (as defined in the Swedish case) may approximate each other more closely than in France.

The questions which arise when we attempt to interpret distance-influences, underline the need for further research on two hypotheses: the divergence of social and physical distance, and the substitution of commuting for migration.

## 1.4  Factors in the development of a migration policy

### 1.4.1  Macro-aspects

Experience in the four countries studied suggests that the foundations of migration policy are usually to be found at the aggregate regional level, although migration aid in the sense of certain financial assistance manifests itself more in the form of more individual and 'social' aid, that is as traditional policies dealing with certain deprived marginal groups in society. However, the aggregate regional view prevails even though, like regional policy, it may be fairly recent in character.

If we should try to evaluate an existing migration policy or develop a new one, we must first consider the magnitude of the problem, which implies that net migration is the starting point of migration policy. And whilst it has been shown that this concept is a second-best one, data availability may mean resort to the second best and, in the short run, there is no alternative but to adapt our techniques to the available regional statistics. In the medium or longer term, of course, statistics may well be adapted to the optimum techniques needed to provide a 'sound' aggregate basis for migration policy. What is meant by a 'sound' basis? Certainly, it implies that the identified movements are as disaggregated as possible, that is trends in directional flows of inter-regional moves are shown by age, occupational and other relevant groups. Also there is a need for an extrapolation of the identified trend, for a prediction of inter-regional labour migration, other things being equal—the latter being explicitly noted. The most important of the *ceteris paribus* is that there is 'no intervention' or more accurately that existing policies bearing upon migration are pursued unchanged. Such a 'conditioned' prediction may either refer to, say, a subsequent period of five or ten years, or to another specific time period, but it may also refer to a hypothetical future state of equilibrium for which Andrei Rogers has already provided examples in his (components-of-change and cohort-survival) techniques for analysing inter-regional population growth and distribution.[64]

Estimating the situation at 'stability', or at 'stationarity', requires the matrix formulation of a country's pattern of inter-regional population growth and distribution. Once a future state, equilibrium or otherwise, at, say, the end of a five-year period, is known it can then be evaluated. Positive or negative net migration as such does not constitute an adequate criterion for determining whether positive or negative net-migration in a region is desirable or undesirable, even if the zero-sum problem, discussed earlier, is left out of account. One must have additional criteria, preferably taken from outside the demographic sphere, and yardsticks of 'good' or 'bad' trends usually are external.

Unfortunately, precise indicators of what is desirable or not are hard to come by. Political pressures do much to explain why the chronic out-migration areas, mostly economically distressed rural or old industrial areas, are usually regarded as the problem areas for purposes of migration policy. And whilst reasons for action to benefit these areas are well supported by statistical indicators, considerably less use is made of such evidence for, say, metropolitan areas where out-migration is desired principally because it is not wanted in the distressed areas. The presence of diseconomies of scale or social costs may constitute legitimate arguments in favour of a policy of net out-migration from dominant metropolitan centres, but often they are accepted as somehow 'self-evident', inducing politicians to dispense with a presentation of the evidence. Thus an evaluation of current trends in inter-regional population distribution often suffers from a regional imbalance of arguments, as well as from a lack of clarity with respect to the criteria applied. Without implying any prejudice for or against distressed or congested (or any other) region, we would like to repeat that an analysis which might broaden the range of criteria and thereby the evaluation process consists of assuring that trends in migration (regardless of whether they are in terms of net-migration, directional flows, matrices of inter-regional population growth and distribution, or whether they are aggregated or disaggregated) are appraised by considering them in the context of regional labour markets. Evaluation could then start with the question: what effect would continuation of present trends have upon the regional supply of labour (ideally not in quantitative but also in qualitative terms), and what, in consequence, would this effect have on regional socio-economic development, taking into account the demand-side of the regional labour market and other factors? In short, migration policy can be rationally evaluated only in

56

the context of a manpower or general development policy, by which a consistent set of political choices is clearly established.

Negative evaluations of migration trends, whether or not they are inconsistent or piecemeal, give rise to proposals for action, to attempts to moderate or even reverse the trend. Positive evaluations can result in action to support or accelerate the trend development. The matrix approach, referred to above, proved to be especially appropriate for the calculation of intervention rates. This, however, is by no means the final step in the formulation of a migration policy—unless it is to be based on trial and error, purely and simply, and therefore is not much concerned with feasibility. Assessing the feasibility of a proposed policy-intervention, is another integral part of a rational migration policy. A simple feasibility test has been applied in the Netherlands[65] to the envisaged regional distribution of population. While the intervention rate has been derived from a reconciliation of the politically desired regional distribution of population (on the basis of the country's concept of physical planning) and the distribution at 'stationarity' (according to Rogers), its feasibility has been determined on the basis of the same parsimonious migration model that we have used to illustrate an aggregate view of inter-regional labour migration.

Other things being equal (regional labour force and inter-regional physical distance), the regional distribution of non-agricultural jobs is the most important single factor bearing upon the feasibility of any attempt to steer a country's directional migration flows. However, the impact of non-agricultural employment upon inter-regional migration, varies from country to country as the test results show. Of course, non-agricultural employment has only been used as a crude indicator (the need for and practicability of further research into this topic having been emphasised) but it seems to approximate closely the force of migration policy that seeks to steer migration by means of primarily, financial incentives to regional industrialisation.

While carrying out feasibility tests prior to any action, to control the efficiency of measures after they have been taken, is a desirable element in the design of a rational migration policy, such an efficiency control requires considerable research effort if it is to be more than just guess-work. Certain preliminary work has been carried out in the field of regional policy.[66] An attempt to assess the impact of financial subsidies on inter-regional migration in Sweden will be presented later. The use of pre-action feasibility tests and post-action efficiency controls implies that a particular view is taken of migration policy, the view of a process procedure[67] in which not only feasibility tests and efficiency controls but also medium term extrapolations, evaluations, interventions, revisions together and the elaboration of long term perspectives or planning horizons, are assumed.

## 1.4.2  Micro-aspects

To design a migration policy at the regional level is one thing, implementing it at the household or individual level is another. In general, it is found that an aggregate formulation of migration policy should precede the design of measures for influencing individual decision-making in a way that the aggregate of such decisions accords with the goals aimed at the regional level. The reason for this is to be found in the fact that job opportunities are usually the most important single attraction for long distance movers. However, job opportunities, or the regional demand for labour, constitute the major target variable of regional policy, which is typically aggregative in nature. Of course migration policy could be intended to help individuals only, that is the essence of migration programmes administered by ministries of social affairs. But once living conditions are to a large extent influenced at the aggregate (regional or national) level, it would be paradoxical if individual or household-centred measures should be concentrated on adaptability to change, without taking into account the impacts of policies which seek to influence aggregates. Training affords a good example. It is readily agreed that people should be trained only for existing jobs or for those available by the end of the training. Similarly, it may be asked why the migration of individuals should be stimulated if no job opportunities are available for them in the receiving regions. Moreover, the success of policies directed at influencing certain aggregates depends very much upon the proper reactions of individuals and households. Experience shows that for subsidies to become effective incentives they must first be used by the target population. This is not as obvious as it might seem and the obvious must be questioned as much in the context of migration policy as elsewhere. Thus, considerations at the regional level must be reconciled with those at the household or individual level, if a solid basis for migration policy is to be established.

Assuming that an intervention at the regional level has been decided upon (for instance, the reduction of net out-migration from distressed rural areas or, less frequently, the deliberate stimulation of out-migration from a dominating urban centre into adjacent regions), then the policy may either seek to guide migration along its course or to reverse its direction at the individual level.

Returning to our model, inter-regional migration is explained by non-agricultural employment, labour force and distance, which might be considered as an explanation of the spontaneous course of migration at the aggregate regional level only. In other words, we found an ecological correlation and although a hypothesis about an individual correlation can be deduced from this ecological correlation, it remains a hypothesis only, and not necessarily a proposition valid for households and individuals simply because it proved to be valid at the regional level. If the 'ecological fallacy' is to be avoided, the question of what a spontaneous course of migration means, must be answered separately for households and individuals by focusing on the respective decision-making processes. Motives and barriers derived from and amenable to survey research, that is empirical concepts, may help to identify the spontaneous course of migration.

To begin with, those who are unmotivated but nevertheless move because they are forced to do so, can be discarded because it seems unrealistic to regard migration policy as constituting a large-scale removal in this sense. We are then left with basically two groups: those motivated and capable of overcoming the barriers to migration (a complete decision to move) and those motivated but blocked by certain barriers (an incomplete decision to move). Since those in the first group (the spontaneous movers) would have moved in any case they do not merit special attention in a migration programme except in so far that their destinations chosen spontaneously do not coincide with the regions preferred from an aggregate perspective. But even then little can be done about this discrepancy. As negative measures are usually inadmissible, one can only try to ensure that in the future the same kind of attractions are present in the preferred regions. One might also try to exclude those who would have in any case moved from the policy's benefits unless it is too expensive to separate these spontaneous movers from the others and unless it is desired to extend aid to all movers, a rather generous approach which seems to have validity in Sweden. But it can also be argued that migration generally implies hardship for which compensation should be given regardless of individual variations in hardship. A more rigorous method is employed in the Canadian manpower mobility programme, which, *inter alia* '...provides a measure of benefits that is consistent with the mobility programme's main economic purpose, i.e. to move workers who would not otherwise have moved to more productive opportunities'.[68] The Canadian case shows that the calculation of the 'degree of spontaneity' is feasible. In other words there are real alternatives for the treatment of those motivated and capable of overcoming barriers.

What of those 'who would not otherwise have moved to more productive opportunities'? To subsidise them, and wait and see how it works, is one answer, though surely not the best one since it involves a process of trial and error. What would seem more fruitful would be to find out why sometimes a desire to move does not lead to subsequent action. Identifying the relevant barriers suggests certain fields of action, although not all types of barriers can be removed by immediate measures. It is necessary to check such factors as: the availability of job opportunities (in quantitative and in qualitative terms); the availability of information about jobs, housing and other opportunities; the health of those in question; their financial resources; the availability of housing opportunities and the operation of the housing market; their skill levels or qualifications; their mentality.

Job opportunities are dealt with by regional policy, although they can be tailored to needs—as shown by the American demonstration projects. Attempts to establish improved inter-regional clearance systems, testify to the opinion that the present state of information (especially about job opportunities) is defective. In practice, migration aid in the four countries under consideration, assumes that a lack of resources is the major barrier to migration, and subsidises some of the migration and related costs. Yet actual movers (group II) are not really the problem group, and the question must be posed whether the generosity of subsidising those who would have moved anyhow can be afforded. We conclude therefore that attention should be directed to those who are motivated to engage in inter-regional migration but are handicapped by various specified barriers (group I). But no mention has been made of two further groups: unmotivated to move to another region, one would have difficulty in moving (group III), the other could move any time it was required (group IVb). This is why we labelled the group 'potential future movers' (Table 1.11).

Table 1.11.

Target Groups for Migration Policy at the Micro-level

|  | Motivated | |
|---|---|---|
|  | yes | no |
| Barriers | yes   I blocked movers | III 'immobiles' or handicapped future movers |
|  | no   II 'would have moved anyhow' | IVa forced movers or |
|  |  | IVb potential future movers |

Experience shows that the constellations of motives and barriers in our classification can be identified empirically. Ascertaining motives involves the 'art of asking why'. It is possible to label a respondent as 'unmotivated to move' only after obtaining detailed information from a labour office consultant. A model for this kind of 'survey', developed in the context of community planning, is termed 'collaborative planning'. It is similar to the collaborative marketing approach which assumes that the consumer is not sure of his exact desires but would be interested in defining them with the help of a skilled counsellor who knows the range of possible alternatives. Nelson W. Foote has contrasted this more advanced marketing approach with the early persuasive or hard sell approach, and the more recent 'listening' or poll-taking approach. The parallels with planning are obvious.[69]

Whatever the complexity of the motives and barriers that are ascertained, it must be remembered that they refer to a given moment in time, and those unmotivated at one point may be motivated at a future time. Only a follow-up study to monitor potential target populations for migration policy will help to determine whether or not constellations of motives and barriers identified at a previous point are unchanged in time. Such a follow-up should embrace both stayers and movers. This would assess, in the case of the first group, just how 'hard' the 'hard core' really is, and in the second case it would provide additional insight into the migration problems for which mobility politicians can provide some help. The objective is to facilitate integration for those who intend to stay in the new location, that is, for the 'permanent movers'. A circular letter distributed by the Swedish labour authorities contains advice about assimilation. Advice and assistance of this kind can be facilitated in two ways.

Firstly, those migrants who are likely to experience adjustment difficulties should be identified before they move and made the major target group for integration aid. It is, of course, possible to be less selective by providing post-move counselling to all permanent (and perhaps even temporary or trial) movers provided that counselling resources are unlimited: where such resources are limited the group which predictably will experience problems should be given priority. Secondly, integration aid, benefits from an indication of the problems with which help is needed, implying that the barriers to integration must be specified.

### 1.4.3 Information requirements

It was stated earlier, that techniques for designing a migration policy at the macro- or the micro-level must usually be adapted to the data available, and this normally implies that these techniques are less than ideal. If individual data are not available, we use aggregate data. If there is no event reporting of migration, as in the Netherlands and Sweden, one resorts to census-survival data, and if directional flows are not known then net migration is used instead. The major weakness of migration data is its lack of disaggregation.

It is for this reason that individual data are generally preferable, whether derived from survey data or from special census samples. In addition, individual data can almost always be aggregated if necessary. Survey data[70] are usually rich in terms of the characteristics of movers and stayers, but limited in scope for such important breakdowns as migration differentials. Individual samples from the census, on the other hand, have sufficient scope, but often lack a wealth of indicators. Of course a census is not primarily intended as a migration study, at least not at the individual or household level. Panel studies are especially needed if migration policy is to be concerned with follow-up and if it is to perform a monitoring function. Such panel studies may assume the form of the Göteborg study, where in-migrants were re-interviewed seven months after they had moved into the region—and this kind of panel can be repeated until ultimately it develops into a study of migration histories.

It is also very important, for the formulation of migration policy, that the 'demography of migration' is integrated into the frame of labour markets or manpower balances. The Swedish Labour Force Survey, appropriately regionalised and extended, promises to provide a practicable solution for this particular problem.

It is useful to draw the attention to a recent development in the United States which bears upon manpower policy in general and labour migration in particular. There, great efforts have been made to compile social indicators on the national level,[71] and similar efforts could be made to obtain *regional* social indicators, including those pertaining to geographical and other forms of labour migration, focusing in general on information about an economy's regional labour sub-markets of a nation. Initial work along lines suggested by Perloff, has already been carried out.[72] Further steps in social reporting should concentrate on Duncan's recommendation concerning the measurement of social change, namely a replication of base-line studies.[73]

## Notes

[1] As this book is intended to be policy-oriented we shall be selective in our references. No attempt has been made to compile a complete bibliography of sources related to geographical labour mobility.

[2] There is evidence that this radius becomes larger with falling communication costs.

[3] This approach was first fully developed by Peter H. Rossi, *Why Families Move. A Study in the Social Psychology of Urban Residential Mobility*, Glencoe 1955.

[4] The term 'forced move' may not always be unambiguous. In the present context 'forced' implies a movement of people who are satisfied with their former locations.

[5] Rossi, op. cit., p. 135.

[6] Bengt G. Runblad: *Arbetskraftens Rörlighet*, Uppsala 1964, pp. 54; 259.

[7] Stouffer pointed to the importance of distinguishing between 'objective' and 'apparent' opportunities when examining migration. (Samuel A. Stouffer, *Social Research to Test Ideas*, Glencoe 1962, pp. 68–112).

8 See Everett M. Rogers, *Diffusion of Innovations*, New York and London 1964 (first ed. 1962).

9 H. Emanuel et al, op. cit.

10 See e.g. Rossi, op. cit.

11 Ibid.

12 Emanuel *et al.*, op. cit.

13 E.g. Rossi, op. cit., pp. 99–122.

14 Great Britain: Amelia J. Harris and Rosemary Clausen, *Labour Mobility in Great Britain 1953–63*, London 1966. Sweden: Torvald Gerger, 'Den Svenska Arbetskraftens Flyttningar I Mitten Av 1960-Talet', Urbaniseringsprocessen 11 (1968). United States: John B. Lansing *et al.*, *The Geographical Mobility of Labour: A First Report*, Ann Arbor 1963.

15 Guy Pourcher, *Le Peuplement de Paris*, Paris 1964. Sven Ove Johansson and Sören Olsson, *Flyttningsströmmens Sammansättning och Flyttningens Förlopp*, Göteborg 1968; also Sven Ove Johansson *et al.*, *Kvarvarande Och Avflyttade*, Göteborg 1969 and Kjell Eriksson, *Flyttning Och Familjeanpassning*, Göteborg.

16 Gunnar Olsson, 'Distance and Human Interaction. A Migration Study', in *Geografiska Annaler* 47B, 1965, p. 10.

17 Op. cit., p. 12. See Robert L. Raimon, 'Interstate Migration and Wage Theory', *The Review of Economics and Statistics* 54, 1962, and Gunnar Olsson, 'Utflyttningarna från Centrala Värmland under 1880-talet', *Meddelanden från Uppsala Universitets Geografiska Institution*, Ser. A, No. 178.

18 Michael J. Greenwood, 'An Analysis of the Determinants of Geographic Labour Mobility in the United States', *The Review of Economics and Statistics* 50, 1968, pp. 188–94.
Migration stocks also play a role in international migration: Maurice Wilkinson, 'European Migration to the United States: An Econometric Analysis of Aggregate Labor Supply and Demand', *The Review of Economics and Statistics* 52, 1970, pp. 272–9.

19 Torsten Hägerstrand, 'Migration and Area', in D. Haunerburg and B. Odering (eds.), *Migration in Sweden: A Symposium*, Lund 1957, pp. 27–158.

20 Note also the coverage of various information channels as indicated by the number of observations $N$.

21 Compare Elihu Katz and Paul F. Lazarsfeld, *Personal Influence. The Part Played by People in the Flow of Mass Communications*, Glencoe 1964 (first ed. 1955).

22 E. M. Rogers, op. cit.

23 Compare Per Kempe, *Arbetslöshet och Geografisk Bundenhet*, Stockholm 1965.

24 For these 'migration differentials' or 'thresholds' see also Peter H.

Morrison, *Theoretical Issues in the Design of Population Mobility Models*, Santa Monica, Cal. 1969.

[25] The same kind of patterns are confirmed by official migration statistics, but it would be too space-consuming to include official migration statistics in this study.

[26] Lansing and Mueller, op.cit., p. 156.

[27] J. B. Cullingworth, *Housing and Labour Mobility*, Paris 1969.

[28] See for instance Sherman J. Maisel, 'Rates of Ownership, Mobility and Purchase', in Real Estate Research Program, University of California (ed.), *Essays in Urban Land Economics*, Los Angeles 1966, pp. 76–108; also Morrison, op.cit.

[29] For a discussion of migration histories see Peter A. Morrison, *Implications of Migration Histories for Model Design*, Santa Monica, Cal. 1970.

[30] Richard F. Wertheimer (ed.), 'The Return to Migration in the United States', in *Inter-University Committee on Urban Economics*, in *Conference Papers*, Presented 11–12 September 1969, Cambridge, Mass.

[31] R. A. Jenness, *Manpower Mobility Programs, A Benefit-Cost Approach*, a paper delivered at the North American Conference on Cost–Benefit Analysis and Manpower Policies, 14–15 May 1969, Madison, Wisc.

[32] Jane A. Abramson, *Rural to Urban Adjustment*, Ottawa 1968.

[33] The reduction of mobility, as opposed to immobility, is not discussed here. Previous references to 'immobility' should not be interpreted as the designation of some kind of personal, life-long, destiny, but only the outcome of a certain constellation of motives and barriers at a certain moment in time. Survey research, unless transformed into panel research, simply produces snap-shots at given points of time.

[34] Once costs and benefits have been defined and formalised it should be possible to measure a lack of motivation in terms of an unfavourable benefit–cost ratio, say benefit/cost $\leqslant 1$.

[35] In this case it should be possible to identify the stayers as those with favourable benefit–cost ratios.

[36] See, for instance, Audrey Freedman, 'Labor mobility projects for the unemployed', *Monthly Labor Review*, June 1968, pp. 56–62.

[37] See Pierre Gremion, *La Mise en Place des Institutions Régionales*, Paris 1965.

[38] See, for instance, Commissariat Général du Plan d'Equipement et de la Productivité, *Le Plan 1966–1970*, Rapport Général de la Commission de la Main-d'Oeuvre, Paris 1966.

[39] Studies of British inter-regional migration dealing with the post- 1965 period can of course avoid this need to reduce the number of regions.

[40] See Anthony Goss, 'Regional Planning and Central Government', *Town and Country Planning*, **36**, 1968, pp. 286–92.

[41] Staatsuitgeverij *Tweede Nota over de Ruimtelijke Ordening in Nederland* (Second Report on Physical Planning in the Netherlands), The Hague 1966.

[42] The island, Gotland, has been excluded because of its exceptional geographical features.

[43] See, for instance, Olov Fahlén, 'En Studie over den Interregionala Migrationen I Arbetsmarknadsstyrelsens A-Regioner', *AMS, Meddelanden från Utredningsbyrån*, 1 (1966).

[44] See Direction Général du Travail et de l'Emploi. Service de l'Emploi, *Les Mouvements Migratoires Interrégionaux de la Population Active Occupée entre 1954 et 1962*, Paris 1967. It is significant that this study was undertaken following the suggestion of the 'Direction Régionale de Lyon', in order to provide the latter with information to guide them in the planning of regional labour exchanges.

[45] For instance, Cicely Blanco, *The Determinants of Regional Factor Mobility*, The Hague 1962; Warren Mazek, *The Efficacy of Labor Migration with Special Emphasis on Depressed Areas'*, Working Paper CURZ2, Institute for Urban and Regional Studies, Washington University, June 1966; Ira S. Lowry, *Migration and Metropolitan Growth: Two Analytical Models*, San Francisco 1966.

[46] See George H. Berts and Jerome L. Stein, *Economic Growth in a Free Market*, New York 1964.

[47] Richard F. Muth, 'Migration: Chicken or Egg?', *Inter-University Committee on Urban Economics* (ed), op. cit.

[48] E.g. Åke Andersson and Rune Jungen, 'Balanced Regional and Sectoral Growth', *Regional Science Association Papers* 26 (1971); 179–206

[49] Ter Heide has chosen economic-geographic areas for the Netherlands. (Hendrik ter Heide, *Binnenlandse Migratie in Nederland*, The Hague 1965). Fahlén's study (op. cit.) relates to Swedish A-regions. Studies of net migration in the United States vary in their regional level from SMSAs (Lowry, op. cit.) and urbanised areas (Muth, op. cit.) to states (Blanco, op. cit.).

[50] It is impossible to avoid the double counting of (frequent) movers when the moving events of a number of successive years are aggregated as in the case of the Dutch and Swedish data.

[51] See the appendix, Tables 1–4.

[52] A number of studies contain bibliography of the state of the art, especially: Lowry, op. cit.; Olsson, op. cit.; Greenwood, op. cit.; Jeffrey Willis, *Population Growth and Movement*, Centre for Environmental Studies, Working Paper 12, London 1968; and Andrei Rogers, *Matrix Analysis of Interregional Population Growth and Distribution*, Berkeley and Los Angeles 1969.

[53] See the classic, Hägerstrand, op. cit.

[54] For example Andersson and Jungen, op. cit.

[55] The model presented above is part of a policy model based in turn upon the matrix approach of Rogers. (See Paul Drewe, *Steps Toward Action-Oriented Migration Research. Regional Science Association Papers* 26 (1971): 145–165).

For further research see Paul Drewe and Humphrey M. Rodgers. *Onderzoek naar Vooruitberekeningsmodellen voor de Interregionale Migratie in Nederland*, Rotterdam 1972 and by the same authors, 'Steps Toward Action-Oriented Migration Research. A Progress Report', *Netherlands Economic Institute Series: Foundations of Empirical Economic Research 1972/5.*

[56] See Tables 5–6 in the appendix.

[57] See Tables 5–6 in the appendix.

[58] See Tables 7–10 in the appendix.

[59] Gunnar Olsson has not only introduced distance as an explanatory factor into the analysis of migration, but has also tried to explain separately the distance moved (Olsson, op. cit.). Approaches that extend beyond the 'physical' concept of distance are Hägerstrand's 'migration fields' (Hägerstrand, op. cit.) and Greenwood's 'migration stocks' (Greenwood, op. cit.; Wilkinson, op. cit.).

[60] See Stouffer, op. cit.

[61] This question has been investigated for example, in the Netherlands for the provinces by Ter Heide (op. cit.) and by Somermeyer (W. H. Somermeyer, *Multipolar Human-Flow Models, Regional Science Association Papers* 26 (1971): 131–44.

[62] In practice, the test is applied to a log transformation of the model set out in section 1.3.4.:
$$\log_{12} M_{ij} = \log \alpha_0 + \alpha_1 \log_0 E_j + \alpha_2 \log_0 L_i - \alpha_3 D_{ij}$$

[63] This means calculating the values of $\delta M_{ij}/\delta E_j$

[64] A. Rogers, op. cit.

[65] Drewe, op. cit.

[66] Norbert Vanhove, *De Doelmatigheid van het Regionaal Beleid in Nederland*, Rotterdam, 1961; James R. Prescott and William C. Lewis, *State and Municipal Locational Incentives: A Discriminant Analysis*, mimeographed paper, Department of Economics, Iowa State University, Ames Iowa 1970. Netherlands Economic Institute, *Kampen en Zwolle na Tien Jaar Stimulering*, Rotterdam 1972.

[67] Drew, op. cit. See also 'Process Planning', Symposium on Programming and the New Urban Planning, *Journal of the American Institute of Planners*, **31**, 1965.

[68] Jenness, op. cit., p. 36.

[69] See David R. Godschalk and William E. Mills, 'A collaborative approach to planning through urban activities', *Journal of the American Institute of*

*Planners* **32**, 1966, A. 86. Also, Nelson W. Foote *et al.*, *Housing Choices and Housing Constraints*, New York 1960, p. 308.

[70] For standards of 'good' survey research, in the context of migration, see section 2.2.

[71] United States Department of Health, Education, Welfare (ed.), *Toward A Social Report*, Washington D.C. 1969; Mancur Olson Jr., 'The Purpose and plan of a social report', *The Public Interest* **15** (1969), 85–97; Bertram M. Gross (ed.), 'Social goals and indicators for American society', *The Annals of the American Academy of Political and Social Science* **371** and **373** (1967); Raymond A. Bauer (ed.), *Social Indicators*, Cambridge, Mass. and London 1967; and Eleanor B. Sheldon and Wilbert E. Moore, *Indicators of Social Change: Concepts and Measurement*, New York 1969.

[72] Harvey Perloff, 'New directions in social planning', *Journal of the American Institute of Planners* **31**, 1965, pp. 297–304; Paul Drewe, *Toward A State-of-the Region Report for Los Angeles*, *A Manpower Account* and *A Population Account*, unpublished manuscripts, School of Architecture and Urban Planning, University of California, Los Angeles, Spring 1970.

[73] Otis Dudley Duncan, *Toward Social Reporting: Next Steps*, New York 1969.

# 2 The Principal Features of Public Aid Programmes for Migration

## 2.1 The rationale of central government programmes

Before describing the frameworks of migration policy in the four chosen countries it is useful to re-emphasise one or two important points about the nature of this policy. The policies focus firstly on migration, not mobility, and secondly not on the migration of all those for whom it seems desirable, but only on the migration of unemployed and key workers in between certain well-defined regions. This restricts the policy to a very narrow field of activities, and (with the exception of Sweden) only a *very* small number of workers are involved annually—roughly not more than one third of one per thousand of the total working population.

Too much should not, therefore, be expected of these policies, and it is even questionable whether extensive description of national programmes in the four countries is worth while. It would seem better to concentrate on the measures that appear desirable for improving migration policy (or for integrating an existing migration policy into a general mobility policy), than, for instance, to compare the levels of certain allowances in the four countries, knowing that they are accorded to an insignificant number of workers. Nevertheless a short description of the four policies is given in order to make a general comparison of their structures. In the following chapters policies are considered in a wider framework.

## 2.2 Migration policy in the Netherlands

### 2.2.1 General

At present migration policy in the Netherlands is dictated, as in Great Britain and France, by the objectives of the regional development policy. Policy has changed over the postwar period from an attempt to eliminate labour surpluses in some specific areas in the eastern and northern parts of the country by means of emigration to any other developing region, into a policy aiming at general equilibrium in the distribution of both economic activities and population. This change in objectives resulted from the view that too heavy a concentration in the urbanised western part of the country would not only be unduly costly in economic terms, but would also have an unfavourable influence on living conditions in that region. A population movement to the less developed northern and eastern parts of the country would not only improve their position but simultaneously would help to avoid further congestion in the urbanised western regions. The instruments to reach these goals are, on the one hand, restriction of further growth in the west, and on the other, financial and other assistance to new and expanding firms in the selected development areas. Additionally, a migration policy was implemented to encourage this movement of industries and population, providing a variety of financial assistance to key workers who move with factories to the development areas as well as to the unemployed who go to these areas. The number of workers affected by this scheme during the period 1960–9 was 1,198 of which roughly 85 per cent were employed before migration (the key workers) and 15 per cent were unemployed. That policy helped 163 unemployed persons or a mere 16 per year! Of the key workers, about 80 per cent came from the western (urbanised) part of the country. In 1968, the average costs per case was $150. It should be noted that the numbers affected by the migration scheme prior to 1960 was considerably larger, since at that stage migration to the Rimcity[1] was also subsidised.

Formally, the regulations stipulate that the migration of any unemployed is subsidised, except the migration of an eligible worker to the Rimcity. Employed people are subsidised only if they have high level jobs and leave the Rimcity, a requirement for both handicapped and eligible workers. Agricultural workers are subsidised when moving into the Rimcity, and to the new polders. In the latter case financial support is given even when the worker is employed and is unlikely to become unemployed.

Such have been the basic characteristics of the migration scheme since 1960. Prior to that, as indicated, movement to the Rimcity was also subsidised. This shows that migration policy in the Netherlands served the objectives of regional development policy during the last decade.

A question which arises is why this policy was applied only to a handful of workers. The answer is hard to find. That the number of key workers is rather small in absolute terms is due to the fact that the number of firms leaving the Rimcity is rather small and because in these cases many key workers prefer to stay in the Rimcity. The large distance-influence on Dutch migration confirms this reaction.

As far as the assisted unemployed are concerned, the total unemployed is in any case rather small and many of them prefer to wait for work in their home region. An anticipation of obtaining such work is supported by government promises to bring jobs to the workers. The more backward the area, the more immobile the population and the more firmly the government promises to take measures promoting the location of new industries there.

Two more recent developments in Dutch mobility policy are quite interesting. First there has been an extension of the (non-financial) assistance given to the employed who want to improve their position. Secondly an inter-regional clearance system has been started in which the various districts inform each other about workers (including higher level workers) looking for a better job; information is transmitted to the larger firms in each region. Whilst the impact of this innovation is as yet marginal, it could develop in a way which is potentially promising from a socio-economic point of view. It is a first step (although taken under some rigid constraints) towards providing a more systematic distribution of information that helps to lead the right man to a better job. It is a policy from which both industry and workers might profit greatly.

### 2.2.2  The situation in certain regions

The current situation has been examined in three regions of the Netherlands: the Noord-Brabant region, the region to the south of the Rimcity; the Rotterdam and Hague region and Friesland.

In Noord-Brabant important structural changes have recently occurred. Both the textile and shoe and leather industries were faced with serious structural problems caused by competition within the Common Market. Firms in these branches were usually family enterprises lacking modern management and with poor marketing performances. Other branches, also, have experienced some difficulties in recent years. Despite a rather rapid upswing in the economy in 1968, the region's economy remains rather weak and in several areas reliance is placed on employment elsewhere, notably in the Rimcity. A large daily flow of commuters, particularly to the Rotterdam port areas, has been the result.

As stated, migration to the Rimcity (including the Rotterdam region) is not subsidised, but in terms of employment opportunities—particularly for the western part of the province—this region is the most important. Subsidies are only given to those migrating to the areas designated as development areas within the province. Such opportunities however are minimal. Moreover, the procedural rules are so cumbersome that it can take months before it is decided whether or not a particular case will benefit from the subsidy. In Noord-Brabant, it is also felt that the administration of the scheme is too complicated and that decisions have to be taken at too high a level.

In the northern province of Friesland the key workers' scheme has some significance for key workers, but none for the migration of the unemployed. Again, this is due to the fact that many well-trained young Frisians, failing to find work in their region, where structure of demand provides more jobs to the lower skill brackets, emigrate to regions where they can use their skills, but not to regions for which migration is assisted financially. In addition, a major weakness of the government's policy to development areas is that it is too unstable, and that consequent changes in the designation of development nuclei makes location there an uncertain matter for entrepreneurs. Location in a development area is not a guarantee that firms will benefit from the assistance programme to the same extent in the future.

The authors were informed that the Rotterdam region faces a shortage of unskilled labour and a surplus of skilled labour, particularly in the service sector. To this extent there is a degree of complementarity with The Hague region, where demand is more for the skilled. The shortage of labour throughout the province of Zuid-Holland (which includes both Rotterdam and The Hague) has led to a considerable immigration of foreign workers. In 1969 there were about 20,000 foreign workers in this province, and in addition there are about 30,000 net daily commuters to the Rotterdam region alone. Such voluntary movements benefit in no way from the migration scheme.

Foreign workers are very mobile and even without any financial assistance move easily to places where work is available. Their employment rate is significantly above the Dutch average—and so is their criminality rate, no doubt as a result of the selection process they undergo before entry.

It would seem that the principles on which the migration schemes are based, although in accordance with the regional industrialisation policy, are so contrary to the natural, spontaneous flows, that the effect of the schemes must be limited.

The decision was recently taken by the Ministry of Social Affairs to initiate a survey[2] of 'geographical inter-regional mobility' in the Netherlands. It is expected that the results will help to formulate a migration policy which is geared to the principle of the regional policy and seeks to promote: the migration of skilled workers from the development areas to the development nuclei within those areas; a retardation of the migration of skilled workers from development areas to the western part of the country; the migration of ex-agricultural workers to the development nuclei; the migration of skilled and key workers from the west to the development nuclei; and the migration of unskilled workers from the development areas to the west.

The object of the study is to discover what measures are necessary to promote the migration flows that are deemed desirable in the national context. It seeks to answer the following five questions: what is the effect of a given measure taken to promote the desired migration flow; is this effect identical for all migrants or are there differences in reactions between different groups; what factors cause potential migrants not to migrate; which measures could help in these cases; and in what ways does the process of adjustment vary in practice?

## 2.3 France

### 2.3.1 General

The provision of assistance to French migrants emerged from the recognition that it might contribute to the supply of qualified workers, as well as giving workers jobs corresponding to their needs. It is recognised that the measures should include assistance to counteract the social inconveniences of a move.

A formal policy was introduced in 1954 with the establishment of the Fonds de Développement Economique et Social (FDES) by the Ministry of Labour, to assist 'victims of industrial transformation'. Help was given to those who could not be re-employed locally and consisted of the reimbursement of travel expenses, the cost of moving furniture and a reinstallation bonus varying with family composition, the importance of the move and the conditions prevailing in the area of destination. Assistance is given to workers who are unemployed as a result of the demise, contraction or conversion of their firm, or by a change in its degree of concentration or specialisation. They are eligible for assistance if no employment opportunities exist in their region and if they accept a job elsewhere that is offered by the employment services or endorsed by those services.

A special committee of the Comité Directeur of the FDES and also the Regional Labour Groups[3] had to advise the Ministry of Labour for each individual case before assistance could be granted. This made the application of the rules extremely slow. In addition, developments in the Paris region led to other adjustments in the policy. The provision of aid to key workers in industries decentralising from Paris was introduced and became a major element in the migration policy. Such assistance was provided only if the industry left the Paris Basin; movements within the Basin were not subsidised.

The Intervention du Fonds National d'Emploi in 1963 also led to a modification of the policy. Whilst the composition of the assistance was left unchanged the amounts were raised and defined in terms of multiples of the minimum hourly wage rates (the *SMIG horaire*). Moreover the procedures were simplified, by allowing the necessary decisions to be taken by the Directeur Régional du Travail et de la Main d'Oeuvre in the region of destination.

Experience with these measures led in 1967 to a doubling of assistance for all categories of workers. Additional forms of help were also offered. Provision now exists for a worker and his wife to make a reconnaissance visit to the potential location if it is more than 100 km from his existing residence. And extra allowances are now available for *double résidence* where proper housing cannot be provided at short notice.

It is felt in France that these measures are good, but that additional provisions would make them even more effective. The creation of a 'national employment exchange', by the National Employment Agency has been suggested. It would seek to provide more information for both workers and employers about the opportunities in their own and other regions and to bring about a situation in which workers earn satisfactory wages for the skills they have to offer.

It would seem therefore that basically the French situation is little different from that in the Netherlands. A decentralisation policy, aiming to prevent further excessive growth in the Paris region, together with the promotion of growth in other regions, essentially determines the structure of the migration scheme. In France the number of workers benefiting from the scheme is again very low: in 1966, 1,288 workers or about 0.6 per cent of the working population, comprising 1,051 key workers and 177 unemployed.

The elements of the scheme are also basically the same in France as in the Netherlands. Assistance is given to the unemployed who move (but not to the Paris region) to jobs offered elsewhere by the employment agencies. It is intended especially for workers whose firms experience a cessation, contraction or conversion of activities, or which have been affected by change in the degree of concentration or specialisation.

Moreover, and this is the more important part of the scheme, assistance is given to higher level personnel, including technicians and engineers, employed by firms that decentralise wholly or partially from Paris to the provinces. The key workers' scheme in France is virtually identical to that applied in the Netherlands, the amounts of assistance being roughly three times as great (the average is $400 per case). Assistance is also given to farmers who leave overpopulated areas and settle in receiving areas. An estimated number of 350 families (1,450 individuals) were affected by this scheme in both 1966 and 1967.

Table 2.1.

Dutch and French Mobility Aid Programmes*

| From \ To | Rest of the country (designated areas) | | | |
|---|---|---|---|---|
| | Employed | | Unemployed | |
| | Key | Non-key | Key | Non-key |
| Paris/Rimcity | X | . | X | X |
| Rest of country | . | . | X | X |

X=assistance provided
.   no assistance provided.
* Migration to Paris (or the Rimcity) is not noted in the table, since it is not assisted.

As in the Netherlands, the question arises why such a small number of workers are affected by the programme. In effect, the answer is the same, namely the operation of two important restrictions: exclusion of the Paris (in the Netherlands, the Rimcity) region; and exclusion of employed non-key workers. The Dutch and French programmes are compared in Table 2.1.

### 2.3.2 The situation in certain regions

For the purpose of the study two regions, Bretagne and the Lille-Cambrai region, were visited; a visit of short duration was also paid to the Vendée.

The foundation of the regional sections of the French national plan is, in principle, the forecasts made for the various regions. These forecasts are based upon regional population growth and also sectoral developments, and are sent to the regional authorities for their comments. In so far as the comments are consistent and compatible with general goals for regional developments they are incorporated in the plan. The regional plans have two objectives: to provide a base for the nation's physical planning; and to reveal the regional pattern of the demand for amenities. This approach is complemented by the policy of the *métropoles d'équilibre* which aims at stimulating the growth of major cities (other than Paris) in order to bring about a more balanced distribution of the French urban population.

Two of these *métropoles d'équilibre* are Rennes in Bretagne and Lille in the Nord region. Bretagne has experienced a rate of fairly constant out-migration of roughly 25,000 per annum, about 1 per cent of total population. Inwards migration was 14,000 during the period 1954–62 and 22,000 between 1962–8. The Bretagne population was 5.76 per cent of the total French population in 1946 and 4.95 per cent in 1968 [5]. Thus it would seem that Bretagne has moved on from a stage of 'passive' emigration—the emigration of unskilled workers who cannot find jobs in their own area and are therefore forced to leave—to the 'active' emigration of qualified people seeking better prospects elsewhere, particularly in the Paris region. Migration inwards has not compensated, either quantitatively or qualitatively, for the effects of this emigration, although this aspect may be improving: [4] 'For the future of the region the problem is not to stop all emigration, mobility being a dynamic economic factor, but to induce an equivalent in-migration quantitatively as well as qualitatively'. [5]

It is important to note that the number of people assisted by migration policy in a move to Bretagne was 125 during 1967 and 1968, or rather more 60 per year, while the total flow of in-migrants during the period 1962–8 was 22,000. Thus the percentage of migrants assisted was less than 3 per cent of the total. Clearly from the point of view of the regional goal of a quantitative and qualitative balance in migration, the scheme's effectiveness is extremely limited.

The Nord Pas de Calais region is a typical region in transition, facing all the difficulties posed by stagnating industrial activities, particularly in the textiles and heavy metal industries. Of 21 French regions its population growth was sixth from the lowest during 1962–8. From being a receiving area, it is now an area from which considerable numbers of workers leave annually. The number of workers entering the region with Fonds National de l'Emploi assistance was only 103 in 1967 and 1968. Those helped to leave totalled 124 during the same period. The incredibly low number of workers involved is striking. It is thought locally that a reason for this is that the regulations are largely unknown and therefore many eligible people fail to benefit from the schemes. Even if the schemes were more widely known, however, it is questionable whether, given their basic limitations, they would be much more effective.

## 2.4  Great Britain

### 2.4.1  General

A major economic problem in Great Britain throughout the postwar period has been the contrast between rapid growth in certain areas, causing congestion and severe labour shortages, and much slower growth or even contractions in others. It has been the policy of successive governments to try to correct this tendency by controlling industrial development in the congested areas and providing incentives for new industry in areas of high unemployment. The emphasis has been increasingly on 'taking the work to the worker', rather than vice versa. It is felt that a continuation of a large net outflow of population from Scotland, Wales and Northern England to the Midlands and the South-East following past tendencies would undermine attempts to develop the former regions and would increase the already severe pressures on housing, transport and land in the latter. Major new initiatives to promote large scale long distance migration are therefore regarded as undesirable.

It is clear that, in Great Britain also, migration policy is greatly influenced by regional policy. Leaving aside training allowances, three schemes are operated in Great Britain:

1. The Resettlement Transfer Scheme.

   This scheme is designed to assist unemployed workers and those about to become redundant, who have poor employment prospects in their home area, to move to jobs in other development areas, either for the purpose of permanent resettlement or as a temporary measure until work becomes available in their home area. The number of beneficiaries under this scheme was 6,344 in the financial year 1969/70 and total payments were £497,800—or £78.5 ($190) per beneficiary. The scheme applies to intra-regional as well as inter-regional transfers anywhere in Great Britain.

2. The Key Workers' Scheme.

This helps employed workers who transfer permanently or temporarily to key posts in units established by their employers in development areas or, since 1970, in 'intermediate' areas. The number of beneficiaries under this scheme was 512 in the financial year 1969/70, total payments being £133,100—or £260 ($620) per case.

3. The Nucleus Labour Force Scheme.

Unemployed workers recruited in high unemployment areas and temporarily transferred to their new employer's parent factory for training are assisted by this scheme. In 1969/70 a total of 402 workers received £20,900—or £52 ($140) *per capita.*

Leaving dependents out of account, the three schemes affected 7,258 workers or 0.03 per cent of the total working population. In addition to such government transfer schemes many nationalised industries and private employers operate schemes for employees whom they wish to transfer to new locations. For example, the National Coal Board has a scheme for assisting employees transferring within the industry, and also on first joining the National Coal Board an eligible applicant qualifies for assistance under the government's Resettlement Transfer Scheme, the NCB supplementing the allowances to raise them to the levels provided by its own scheme. Industrial civil servants who transfer are helped in a similar fashion if they agree to serve at the new station for at least two years.

### 2.4.2 The situation in certain regions

Two regions were visited: the North (special attention being paid to Sunderland) and the South-East (focusing on Luton, a town roughly 60 km north of London). The Northern region, with a concentration of coal mines and shipbuilding, has an unemployment rate well above the national average. Sunderland lies on the east coast and suffers from high unemployment and limited employment prospects. The region (including Sunderland) loses a considerable number of workers to the more prosperous areas of the country where employment prospects are better but the number benefiting from any of the above schemes is small. It was felt in the region that the potential migrant is primarily interested in the wage he could earn elsewhere, generally being disinterested in jobs offering less than £20 per week. Housing comes second, even for the single man. If potential earnings and housing are thought to be satisfactory, than the transfer allowance scheme comes into the reckoning for those relatively few who know of it. (Workers in Sunderland do seem to be aware of its existence.)

As one of its functions, the employment exchange arranges for employers from other areas to use its premises for interviewing potential employees. In many cases workers accept job offers at the interview, but in some cases they visit the factory and decide upon the offer after seeing the location and the working conditions. Despite such preparation and the assistance available, a relatively large number of those emigrating return home relatively quickly, domestic difficulties being cited as the major cause of this reaction.

The South-Eastern region offers a sharp contrast to the North. It is a region of high overall employment with an unemployment rate well below the national average. In Luton, a significant proportion of the town's labour force is employed in making vehicles at the Vauxhall works and the general dominance of manufacturing has led to a shortage of skilled and semi-skilled production workers (and a lack of work for women factory workers)—a problem in many parts of the South-East, particularly in areas bordering on Greater London. It was noticeable that a large number of migrant workers in Luton benefited from the Resettlement Transfer Scheme. This may not be so surprising when account is taken of the fact that for the first time we found a significant subsidised flow between a stagnating area and a fast-growing area.

The main difficulty in Luton concerns housing. According to the local authority, an incoming migrant is placed on the accommodation waiting-list only after a stay of two years and he might have to wait a further 1.5 years before obtaining a local authority dwelling. It is estimated that 75 per cent of in-migrants return home within one year and that 50 per cent return in the first month. The Vauxhall works do not consider it their responsibility to provide housing for their employees.

## 2.5   Sweden

### 2.5.1   General

In Sweden, the relationships between regional and migration policy are different from those in any of the other countries studied.

> Obviously, to attain balance on the labour market is not the only aim of labour market policy. Its first aim is to assist individuals to find the kind of work which gives them maximum economic and personal satisfaction. Employment service, vocational guidance and vocational

77

training represent the main implements here but the attempts to locate firms in areas which have a manpower surplus represent one important complement to the mobility promoting policy.[6]

Although there is a tendency to place increasing emphasis on regional policy measures—new legislation was enacted in 1970—it appears that in Sweden regional policy is regarded as a complement to migration policy and this in turn is essentially a mobility policy.

It is unlikely that a major reason for this approach is the fact that urban areas in Sweden are appreciably smaller than in the three other countries so that the further expansion of the Stockholm and Göteborg areas for instance is seen in a different light from the growth of the London, Paris and Rimcity areas. In consequence movements to the main urban areas are also subsidised in Sweden and much larger numbers thereby benefit from the schemes. This can be shown by the following figures. Most assistance is given in the form of 'starting help' and in the financial year 1967/68 22,468 persons benefited from this assistance. Of those 8,287 (or 37 per cent) moved to the urban areas of Stockholm, Göteborg and Malmö, while 6,060 people (29 per cent) moved within their region. About one third of the movers lived in the relatively underdeveloped northern regions of Västerbotten and Norrbotten, and of these about a third again moved within their region.

Even allowing for the fact that migration to urban areas is also subsidised in Sweden and for the fact that the country's low population density makes it desirable to change location more often as a consequence of a job change, these figures, in relation to the total population, are nevertheless remarkable. A statistical test[7] has revealed the effectiveness of the Swedish subsidy system, by showing that the number of migrants, particularly from the northern regions, is higher than could be expected without subsidy. Thus migration policy in Sweden contrary to that in the other countries (including Great Britain), helped considerably to solve the unemployment problem in lagging regions. Both the structure of the policy and the subsidy level have contributed to this achievement.

The programmes include the following items:

In accordance with the Labour Market Ordinance, transfer grants are available under certain conditions, for unemployed persons who are unable to find a job in or near their place of residence and who must therefore move to another locality. The allowances available include *travelling allowances* (to seek and take up employment or for the removal of the family and the transport of household goods), a *starting allowance* (for expenses during the initial period in the new employment) and a *separation allowance* (for breadwinners who have to maintain two house-holds). Moreover, an *equipment allowance* is available for families who move from areas with particularly high and persistent unemployment to take up employment in another area. The starting allowances amount-ed to a maximum of Sw.Kr. 500 ($100). The allowance for the spouse or housekeeper was Sw.Kr. 220 ($44) and the allowance for each child Sw.Kr. 60 ($12) a month. The maximum housing allowance was Sw.Kr. 300 ($60) a month and the family allowance was payable for a maximum of twelve months. The equipment allowance amounted to Sw.Kr. 2,000 ($400) plus Sw.Kr. 150 ($30) for each child. The Labour Market Board was also able to grant breadwinners affected by seasonal unemployment a special family allowance. This amounted to Sw.Kr. 300 ($60) a month during a maximum of six months and was intended to make it easier for the seasonally unemployed to take a job in another area while waiting to return to their ordinary work in their home district.[8]

Clearly, the Swedish programmes affect a much larger proportion of the working population—6 per cent—than the schemes in the other countries. Apart from the explanations already put forward, it seems likely that this difference is partly due to the more favourable terms and to the fact that assistance is not limited to those moving to development areas.

### 2.5.2 The situation in certain regions

Visits were paid to Norrbotten and Göteborg, the former being a departure area, the latter a receiving area.

The size of the Norrbotten region is 99,000 km², most of it in the Arctic Circle. It has a population of 257 thousand. Luleå, an industrial and ad-ministrative centre on the Baltic coast with 58 thousand inhabitants, and Kiruna, a mining town in the Arctic Circle with 29 thousand inhabitants, are the only expanding towns in the region.

Labour requirements in agriculture, which is based upon smallholdings and forestry, are rapidly declining. The demand for labour in mining and the pulp and paper industry, comparatively large employers in the region, is stagnating. Other non-agricultural employment has not expanded enough to compensate for these developments and the natural growth of the popula-tion. Therefore Norrbotten has for some time been an out-migration region. In the period 1960–8, net out-migration amounted to 24,300 a figure equiv-alent to more than 9 per cent of the size of the population at the beginning of the decade. The unemployment rate is higher than in any other region: in October 1969, 11.5 per cent of the total number of unemployed persons were in Norrbotten compared with 3.2 per cent of the country's total population.

The government has tried to attract new industry to the region. Public work projects, with the immediate objective of providing work for the unemployed have also been chosen with a view to improving the region's infrastructure and thereby facilitating industrial expansion. The ironworks at Luleå, employing 3,500 persons, is a government undertaking established in 1940. Norrbotten is in a development area that is accorded special preference for industrial location subsidies. However, it is clear that these measures have not been sufficient for securing employment for more than a small part of the region's labour surplus.

In accordance with the national mobility policy, the regional labour market authorities offer work applicants jobs in central and southern Sweden together with economic assistance to seek and take up employment there, provided that there are no satisfactory employment opportunities available within the region. Information about job opportunities, national in coverage is provided by the national employment service system. One of the information media, the weekly *Labour Market Journal*, listing about 16,000 unfilled vacancies and providing particulars about the work, wages and housing facilities etc., is available at all employment offices.

An important aid to the employment of migrating workers is the provision of vocational training under the aegis of the general training scheme for labour market purposes. Such training can be given in Norrbotten or in the receiving area. Employment exchanges in the north liaise with their counterparts and also with individual undertakings, in the south. The latter send recruitment officers to Norrbotten to inform those seeking work at employment offices about work conditions, training facilities, housing, etc. in the receiving areas.

In addition, attempts have been made to develop the Luleå–Piteå–Boden area as a coastal growth pole, but its prospects are not too bright. It is expected that, if present conditions persist, Norrbotten's population will decrease from 260,000 to 195,000 in 1980. It is possible therefore that in the future stronger measures will be taken to create jobs in the region itself, especially in the coastal area.

It is felt that the most difficult problems facing emigrants from the area are those of housing and integration in the receiving area. Solutions of these problems are considered to be government and trade union tasks, though the assimilation problem is also understood at the Volvo works in Göteborg.

Working conditions in the large factories in Göteborg are very different from those in rural areas or small towns, and housing difficulties, together with a sense of isolation in the big city, make integration difficult.

Assistance starts at the place of recruitment. Contacts with the employment officer are good. Volvo recruitment officers frequently visit both smaller and larger towns in the north. For those who are interested, films about training and retraining centres are shown. Brochures about the Volvo works and Göteborg are distributed together with the necessary information about salaries and accommodation—apartment, hotel or hostel. Visits to Göteborg can be arranged for workers and their wives, if requested. Travel expenses and daily allowance are paid.

Volvo representatives drew attention to the fact that many young workers from Norrbotten wish to return home in the spring to help on the family farm, coming back to Göteborg in the autumn. During this period they are often replaced by students. This might be avoided by attracting more complete families, but this, in turn, requires more houses. Volvo representatives also thought it desirable to exercise influence over the choice of training course via the Employment Offices. The major problem in Göteborg (and in Stockholm too) is the housing problem. There has been a housing shortage since 1940 and although residential hotels and hostels have been built (and even ships have been converted into dwellings) the housing shortage nevertheless remains a major reason why people return to their region of origin. Conditions are even worse for foreign workers in Göteborg.

An additional consideration is the high cost of accommodation and of the daily journey to work. An estimate of the average yearly rent for a new three-room apartment in Göteborg is Sw.Kr. 5,000 in contrast to an average rent for a less modern apartment or house in Norrbotten of not more than Sw.Kr. 1,000. Daily travel costs in Göteborg might total Sw.Kr. 600 to 700 per year. Thus net spendable income in Göteborg, where gross income is about Sw.Kr. 25,000 for an automobile worker could even be less than in Norrbotten, where gross income is estimated to be Sw.Kr. 20,000 for a seasonal forestry worker. Moving south may, however, have advantages in terms of family income, since Göteborg offers more job opportunities for women than Norrbotten, as well as more stability of employment and better prospects for children.

It is believed that the most difficult problem facing emigrant workers from Norrbotten is that of housing and integration in the area of destination. The official attitude to this problem is expressed in a memorandum issued by the National Labour Board to employers, local unions and municipal authorities. In the Board's view, integration is a matter of concern for each of the three parties as well as for the employment service. The memorandum gives detailed guidance to each party about the kind of action needed to improve the position of the migrant workers. However, there is still much that can be done in this connection.

**Notes**

[1] The ring of larger cities in the western part of the country.

[2] To be carried out by the Institute for Applied Sociology at Nijmegen, Holland.

[3] Groupe régional de travail.

[4] Alain Even, *Evolution de la population en Bretagne depuis 1962*, Centre Régional d'Etudes et de Formation Economiques, Rennes, 1969.

[5] Op. cit., 2.10, and 12 respectively.

[6] A.M.S. Berättelse. *Budgetåret 1967–68*, p. 116.

[7] Compare the appendix, Tables 11–13.

[8] A.M.S. Berättelse *Budgetåret 1967-68*, p. 128. The above rates have subsequently been raised.

# 3 Evaluation of Programmes

## 3.1 Introduction

Since the programmes considered have been adjusted to, or have emerged from, the particular situations in each country, their details can only be judged in relation to all these formative factors. Such an evaluation is not, however, the object of this chapter. Rather than focusing on the details of programmes which (with the exception of Sweden) affect very small numbers of people, we prefer to discuss the broad outlines of these programmes in the light of the conclusions of preceding chapters that dealt with both theoretical and practical aspects. The knowledge accumulated in these chapters permits the formulation of certain basic conditions against which the outline of existing programmes can be judged.

The conditions and assumptions are:

1. That the mobility of labour and capital are virtues in themselves. Education and information are instruments for reaching a higher level of mobility in the case of both, and are conducive to better judgements on the basis of improved information.

2. Both migration policy and regional policy would be superfluous if; labour and capital were perfectly mobile; and these mobilities resulted in the flows of labour and capital thought desirable in the national context.

3. If the latter condition is not fulfilled, migration policy needs to be selective, that is it must use instruments which adjust private decisions to national objectives in cases where such a reconciliation is needed.

4. Corrections to private economic decisions could be made by attaching subsidies to desired moves and taxes to undesired moves. In practice, only the first instrument is used—though in Sweden, special economic measures to curb building investments in overexpansive areas are currently under consideration.

5. In order to make a corrective and selective policy effective, three kinds of data are needed: how, and on the basis of what information, are private decisions taken; what is the 'net profit' of such a decision; and given this

amount, what is the proper incentive for correcting the decision. In principle these three elements constitute the result of a private cost–benefit analysis.

6. In order to appraise the national economic desirability of such a correction, the size of the necessary incentive needs to be compared with the national economic advantage which the sought-after decision has over the private decision. Only in cases where the national cost–benefit analysis suggests a surplus greater than or equal to, the subsidy's national economic impact, should the incentive be provided.

These six considerations must be kept in mind when considering the outlines of the existing programmes.

However, before evaluating the programmes in this way, it is useful to pursue in further detail some general aspects of cost–benefit analysis, since certain points need to be elaborated before a proper policy evaluation is possible.

## 3.2   Cost-benefit analysis of migration

### 3.2.1   *Private economic cost-benefit analysis*[1]

Let us assume that an individual[2] lives in region $i$ and considers migrating to region $j$. His present income is $y_i(0)$ and expected future income for the year $t$ is $y_i(t)$, both measured in real terms. By moving from $i$ to $j$ the individual could improve his income prospects in year $t$ to $y_j(t)$, also measured in real terms by correcting for eventually higher living costs in $j$. Thus his net gain for year $t$ by moving from $i$ to $j$ would be $y_j(t)-y_i(t)$ and the present value of the income increases

$$B_E^{ij} = \int_0^{\lambda} \{y_j(t)-y_i(t)\}\, e^{-\rho t}\, dt \tag{3.1}$$

where $\lambda$ is the number of years over which it is expected that the higher income will be earned, and $\rho$ is the subjective discount rate. Clearly $\lambda$ and therefore the net gain to be obtained from migration, is lower for older people. In consequence, it may not be strictly true to say that older people are necessarily less mobile than young people. We simply know that if all circumstances *other than age* are constant, the elderly move less. But, as shown, a reason for this is that the incentive proves to be less sharp for them than for younger people. We may well say, therefore, that they migrate less than younger people for very good reasons. Whether or not they are inherently less mobile than younger people can only be ascertained after correcting for the difference in the impact of the incentive (the present value of the future income differential).

The benefits in Equation (3.1) represent only economic—or, more precisely, financial—benefits. A move from $i$ to $j$ might, however, also give rise to benefits non-economic in nature. Pleasanter surroundings, an urban life and more adequate social amenities etc. might constitute further arguments for moving. The 'present value' of these social benefits will be shown as $B_S^{ij}$. Total benefits are therefore $B_E^{ij} + B_S^{ij}$. Costs, basically, fall into the same two categories. First there are the financial costs of moving, and installation in new accommodation and travel costs etc. These costs, which are a function of the distance moved, are given by $C_E(A_{ij})$.

The social 'costs' reflect those sacrifices which a person makes when leaving the region and neighbourhood where he has social ties with family and friends. These costs are also an increasing function of distance. The sacrifice of abandoning social ties is greater the further the individual or household moves and the higher the communication costs become. Unfavourable housing conditions in the receiving area should also be included with these costs, which are denoted by $C_S(A_{ij})$.

It follows that, by definition, the net gain of the individual is:

$$G_{ij} = B_E^{ij} + B_S^{ij} - C_E(A_{ij}) - C_S(A_{ij}) \tag{3.2}$$

a gain which is evidently a decreasing function of distance. The individual will migrate from $i$ to $j$ if $G_{ij}$ is positive and larger than for any other $j$.

Consider a possible move of the individual from $i$ to $k$, instead of to $j$, where his gain would be $G_{ik}$. In order to change his choice from $j$ to $k$, a subsidy, larger than $G_{ij} - G_{ik}$, should be offered to him. Thus

$$S > G_{ij} - G_{ik} \tag{3.3}$$

or

$$S > B_E^{jk} + B_S^{jk} + \{C_E^{ik} - C_E^{ij}\} + \{C_S^{ik} - C_S^{ij}\} \tag{3.4}$$

In other words, the subsidy should exceed the sum of: the economic benefits of $j$ in so far as these exceed those of $k$; the social 'benefits' of $j$ in so far as these exceed those of $k$; the difference in economic costs of moving from $i$ to $k$ and from $i$ to $j$; and the difference in social 'costs' of moving from $i$ to $k$ and from $i$ to $j$.

If $k$ is further from $i$ than $j$, the third and fourth elements will be positive, otherwise negative. The following important conclusions may now be drawn: the subsidy should be dependent upon the age of the individual; it should be larger the greater the distance which individuals are to move compared with the distance they would have covered spontaneously; it should also depend on the income differential between the spontaneous and the desired move. Thus subsidies should be differentiated according to age, and the location of the potential migrant.

### 3.2.2 Macro-economic cost-benefit analysis

The macro-economic calculations are considerably more complicated than those for the individual. When considering an individual's decision, and calculating the incentive needed to change it, we could ignore whether or not this incentive accorded with the national economic advantage. This question, however, is in the macro-economic context.

First consider the cost to the economy of granting the subsidy. For simplicity we assume that the individual can use the subsidy for consumption or saving, the latter being regarded as a contribution to future income, the former not. This, of course, is a simplification, but even with it the problem is complicated enough. For the government, the two alternatives are consumption and investment.

Now suppose that the individual's propensity to save is $\sigma_P$ and that $\sigma_G$ represents the government's marginal investment propensity. If the savings of the individual result in investment, then the subsidy's impact on national investments is

$$\Delta I = (\sigma_P - \sigma_G)\, S \tag{3.5}$$

and $\Delta I$ is negative for $\sigma_P < \sigma_G$, which can be safely assumed in this case.

If the marginal capital-output coefficient is $\kappa$, then the resulting annual loss in income is:

$$\Delta Y = \frac{1}{\kappa}\, \Delta I = \frac{1}{\kappa}\, (\sigma_P - \sigma_G)\, S \tag{3.6}$$

and the total income loss after correction for the lower level of consumption in the year the subsidy is given

$$\Delta Y_T = \int_0^\infty \frac{1}{\kappa}\, \Delta I e^{-rt}\, \mathrm{d}t - (\sigma_P - \sigma_G)\, S$$

$$= \frac{1}{r\kappa}\, \Delta I - (\sigma_P - \sigma_G)\, S$$

$$= \frac{\sigma_P - \sigma_G}{r\kappa}\, S - (\sigma_P - \sigma_G)\, S = \frac{\sigma_P - \sigma_G}{r\kappa}\, S\,(1 - r\kappa) \tag{3.7}$$

where $r$ is the objective discount rate (the long-term rate of interest) and $\sigma_P - \sigma_G / r\kappa$ the subsidy effect.

This is not the complete story, however. An important consideration is that the government values income produced at $j$ and $k$ differently from the individual. There are several reasons for this. Firstly, prices and taxes in different regions do not reflect real costs in those regions, so that a given real income for the individual can have a different value for the government—or rather for the nation as a whole. Secondly, the authorities attempt to bring about a more balanced geographical population distribution. Although this objective is seldom expressed formally or precisely, it implies that unduly large conurbations are to be avoided in favour of middle-sized cities in other parts of the country. To some extent this consideration reflects the preceding factor but it also plays an independent role.

Finally, income may not be the only decisive element in the geographical distribution of economic activity. A concentration of industrial activities might result in the deterioration of the whole environment of the region in question, while more dispersal would moderate such an effect.

In the present context these considerations can best be introduced as a correction to each region's income. If real income—as defined earlier—for the individual in region $i$ is $y_i$, we may define the macro-economic evaluation of $y_i$ as $\gamma_i y_i$ where $\gamma_i$ is the correction factor. This factor will exceed unity for those areas where growth is considered desirable, and be less than unity if the region's growth is thought undesirable.

Reconsidering the decision of the individual for whom there was an economic benefit of $B_E^{ij}$ in moving from $i$ to $j$

$$B_E^{ij} = \int_0^{\lambda} \{y_j(t) - y_i(t)\}\, e^{-\rho t}\, dt \tag{3.1}$$

we find that the macro-economic benefit of such a move is

$$B_{EM}^{ij} - \int_0^{\lambda} \{\gamma_j y_j(t) - \gamma_i y_i(t)\}\, e^{-rt}\, dt \tag{3.8}$$

There are thus three elements in Equation (3.8) that differ from Equation (3.1), namely the objective discount rate, which replaces the subjective rate, a new evaluation of income in $i$, and of income in $j$. If $r = \rho$, $\gamma_j > 1$ and $\gamma_i < 1$, $B_{EM}^{ij}$ could be considerably larger than $B_E^{ij}$.

If we suppose that the macro-social benefits and costs are also incorporated in the income correction, the limits for the subsidy may be prescribed. From the national economic point of view a subsidy is justified if the macro-economic benefits of a change in the decision to move from $i$ to $j$, instead from $i$ to $k$, exceed the costs of the change, that is if

$$B^{ik}_{EM} - B^{ij}_{EM} > \frac{\sigma_G - \sigma_P}{r\kappa} S(1 - r\kappa)$$

or

$$S < \frac{r\kappa}{\sigma_G - \sigma_P}(1 - r\kappa)(B^{ik}_{EM} - B^{ij}_{EM}) \tag{3.9}$$

We earlier concluded, that in order to induce the individual to change his decision, Equation (3.3) must be fulfilled, that is

$$S > G_{ij} - G_{ik} \tag{3.3}$$

Together the two requirements result in a single condition

$$G_{ij} - G_{ik} < S < \frac{r\kappa}{\sigma_G - \sigma_P}(1 - r\kappa)(B^{ik}_{EM} - B^{ij}_{EM}) \tag{3.10}$$

which implies that the subsidy should simultaneously satisfy two conditions: it must be larger than the loss in benefit, caused by the individual switching his decision from $j$ to $k$; and be less than the net gain for the economy as a whole, when corrected for the marginal impact of the subsidy on the economy.

It may be noted that if $\sigma_G = \sigma_P$, the condition for $S$ is such that it could be infinitely large. This merely reflects the fact that transferring money from the government to an individual is not a cost to the nation as a whole if the two spending patterns are identical.

If these two conditions are not satisfied, implying that no positive value for $S$ fulfils condition (3.10), the subsidy is not justified. The reasons for this are clear. If the changed decision entailed a national economic benefit, but the subsidy was not large enough to induce the change, the subsidy would be meaningless. No more is it justified if it results in a changed decision which although beneficial from a private point of view, would result in a national economic loss.

A more simple interpretation of Equation (3.10) is that a subsidy is justified if, and only if, the private loss resulting from altering a decision to move from $i$ to $j$ to one to move from $i$ to $k$ is more than offset by the macro-economic gains stemming from such a decision corrected for the subsidy effect.

All aspects are not yet covered. It was assumed above that the subsidy was given to anyone who changes his decision as a result of the subsidy. But the government is unable to discriminate between those who would in any event have decided to move from $i$ to $k$ and those who changed their decision. The subsidy will have to be paid to both. If the number changing their decision because of the subsidy is $r$, and the number who move spontaneously from $i$ to $k$ is $s$, then the total number of subsidies is $1+r/s$ times the number changing their decision. The macro-economic costs of the superfluous subsidies are the same as for the required ones but since there are no returns to these subsidies, condition (3.10) becomes

$$G_{ij} - G_{ik} < S < \frac{r\kappa}{\sigma_G - \sigma_P} (1 - r\kappa) (B_{EM}^{ik} - B_{EM}^{ij}) \frac{r}{r+s} \qquad (3.11)$$

where $r$ is the number of induced movers and $s$ is the number of spontaneous movers. This additional condition appreciably narrows the range in which $S$ may lie and consequently limits the number of cases where it is desirable, in a macro-economic context, to pay a subsidy. This condition is both *necessary* and *sufficient*.

We may round off these conditions by reformulating (3.11) in terms of subsidy effectiveness.
If

$$\varepsilon_P = \frac{S}{G_{ij} - G_{ik}} \qquad (3.12)$$

is called the private effectiveness of the subsidy and

$$\varepsilon_G = \frac{B_{EM}^{ik} - B_{EM}^{ij}}{\dfrac{(\sigma_G - \sigma_P)(1 - r\kappa)}{r\kappa}} \cdot \frac{r}{r+s} \qquad (3.13)$$

is termed its macro-economic effectiveness, than condition (3.11) is fulfilled if, simultaneously,

$$\varepsilon_P, \varepsilon_G > 1 \qquad (3.14)$$

### 3.2.3 Application to the unemployed

Turning now to the case where the subsidy is given to an unemployed individual, the following modifications need to be introduced.
1. Equation (3.1) becomes

$$B_E^{iju} = \int_0^{\tau'} \{y_j(t) - y_i^u(t)\} e^{-\rho t} dt + \int_\tau^\lambda \{y_j(t) - y_i(t)\} e^{-\rho t} dt \qquad (3.15)$$

so that the net profit of moving from $i$ to $j$ consists of the present value of the difference between the income to be earned at $j$ and the unemployment payment at $i$ during the anticipated period of unemployment $\tau$, increased by the present value of the income differential between $j$ and $i$ over the period $\tau - \lambda$.

The difference between (3.15) and (3.1) is the present value of the difference between regular income in $i$ and the unemployment payment during the estimated time of unemployment. We denote this by $Y_i - Y_i^u$.

2. $B_S^{ij}$ is unchanged, as are $C_E(A_{ij})$ and $C_S(A_{ij})$.

3. Equation (3.2) becomes

$$G_{ij}^u = G_{ij} + Y_i - Y_i^u \tag{3.16}$$

For region $k$, (3.16) becomes

$$G_{ik}^u = G_{ik} + Y_i - Y_i^u$$

so that

$$G_{ij}^u - G_{ik}^u = G_{ij} - G_{ik} \tag{3.17}$$

and condition (3.3) thus remains unchanged.

Equation (3.5) is not affected but there will be an additional benefit for the government equal to $Y^{u'}$.[3] The contribution of this to investment is $(\sigma_G - \sigma_P)Y^{u'}$ and to income $\sigma_G - \sigma_P/r\kappa \; Y^{u'}(1 - r\kappa)$.

However, this benefit is independent of whether the migrant goes to $j$ or to $k$. Since, therefore, no benefit is derived from a change in decision from $j$ to $k$, the final conclusions remain unchanged.

One might consider the case not of a change decision, but merely whether there should be migration or not.[4] In this case both equation (3.15) and (3.16) are valid. Writing (3.16) in full, we have

$$G_{ij}^u = B_E^{ij} + B_S^{ij} - C_E(A_{ij}) - C_s(A_{ij}) + (Y_i - Y_i^u) \tag{3.18}$$

The individual will migrate spontaneously if, and only if, $G_{ij}^u > 0$. If $G_{ij} < 0$ a subsidy, $S > G_{ij}^u$, is needed to induce him to migrate. If such a subsidy is paid, the cost is as before:

$$\frac{\sigma_G - \sigma_P}{r\kappa} (1 - r\kappa)$$

However, unemployment benefits, totalling $Y^{u'}$ are saved which, in the national-economic context, means a switch from private spending (with a savings ratio $\sigma_P$) to government spending (with a savings ratio $\sigma_G$). The costs of the subsidy are thus reduced to:

$$\frac{\sigma_G - \sigma_P}{r\kappa} (S - Y^{u'})(1 - r\kappa)$$

The national-economic gain in income stemming from the migration of the worker from $i$ to $j$ equals $B_{EM}^{ij}$, so that the subsidy is justified if, and only if:

$$B_{EM}^{ij} > \frac{\sigma_G - \sigma_P}{r\kappa} (S - Y^u) (1 - r\kappa) \qquad (3.19)$$

from which it follows:

$$S < \frac{r\kappa}{(\sigma_G - \sigma_P)(1 - r\kappa)} B_{EM}^{ij} + Y^{u'} \qquad (3.20)$$

Thus, the subsidy should thus be less than the corrected macro-economic benefits plus the savings on employment payments, in other words the subsidy amount $Y^{u'}$ could be larger than in the case of an employed worker.

The necessary and sufficient condition is:

$$G_{ij}^u < S < \frac{r\kappa}{(\sigma_G - \sigma_P)(1 - r\kappa)} B_{EM}^{ij} + Y^{u'} \qquad (3.21)$$

and this is fulfilled in all cases where the national-economic net benefits exceed the private economic net benefits.

### 3.2.4 Return movements

We have not yet examined the implications of a return of the migrant to his home area. Experience in the four countries suggests that the number of such returns is considerable and it is a factor which should be introduced in the cost–benefit analysis.

A large number of returns is a result either of a bad evaluation of the situation or of lack of information or both. The number of return movements can therefore be reduced if an effective mobility policy is pursued. As previously stated, such a mobility policy should concentrate on the supply of precise and complete information, and also the provision of education adequate enough to enable more people to assess realistically the situation in receiving areas. It would seem that the judgement factor is even more significant than the provision of information. A high proportion of workers who migrated to Luton returned because of the poor housing accommodation, though they had been well warned in advance. Experience gained during their stay soon changed their decision and led to a return.

The general condition (3.11) we formulated earlier in this chapter is evidently not affected by these considerations. To understand this, it is sufficient to recall that the condition holds under the assumption that the higher income or higher social satisfaction would be obtained over a period of $\lambda$ years, and this period was not explicitly stated. Formally, therefore, the analysis is unaffected. Nevertheless, the absolute size of the estimated private net benefits is a decreasing function of the number of years over which these benefits apply and it is true for the macro-economic benefits. In other words, the range in which the subsidy may lie is dependent upon the factor $\lambda$: the smaller $\lambda$, the more will the range shift to lower values for the subsidy.

At this stage an interesting question arises: in what form should the subsidy be given? It is usually provided *à fonds perdu*, that is paid in full after the move. It is not difficult however to prescribe two alternative forms which offer much more flexibility for adjustment to the actual length of stay in the receiving area.

The first possibility would be to pay the subsidy in instalments, over a period of say three years. (In Sweden a period of six months is the rule after which the likelihood of a return is negligible.) Secondly it is possible to regard the subsidy as a loan that must be repaid if the return takes place earlier than anticipated.

Administratively both proposals (but especially the second) are more complicated than a subsidy *à fonds perdu*. Even so the savings might be larger than this increase in costs, particularly in cases such as Luton where the return movements are so overwhelmingly large.

If subsidies continue to be provided in their existing form and under existing rules then it should be appreciated that in effect some compromise solution is being accepted. Those emigrating definitely receive a subsidy below a reasonable amount and the returns receive something above the amount justified. Thus, it would seem desirable to contemplate the introduction of a more flexible subsidy system along the lines suggested above.

### 3.2.5 Inter-relationships

One factor is still to be considered: the repercussions of the subsidy system on regional labour surpluses or shortages. By transforming potential movers from $i$ to $j$ into actual movers from $i$ to $k$, the labour market in both $j$ and $k$ is affected. An assumption that this changed decision will not affect wage differentials between $j$ and $k$ would conflict with the model presented in section 0.3.2. However, this complication is not introduced at this stage.

It would be useful if the consequences of a migration policy for the regional labour markets were to be studied more carefully. Testing of the model presented in the Introduction might constitute a start for the study. However, such a study and such a test are beyond the scope of this study.

### 3.3 Actual policies (general evaluation)

If actual policies are compared with the theoretical findings of the first two sections of this chapter, a number of interesting points emerge.

(a) Actual subsidies do not vary with income differentials or with distances— though the size of transportation costs depends on distance.

(b) Subsidies do not vary with the age of the migrant or his length of stay in the receiving area. (Except in the case of starting help in Sweden.)

(c) In practice, subsidies are based neither on private nor macro cost– benefit analyses. The level of the subsidies is based essentially on *Fingerspitzengefühl*, and the outcome of such 'verbal calculations' may not be very reliable. Evidence of the use of this methodology is to be found in the periodic, but arbitrary, increases in subsidies, sometimes by as much as 100 per cent. Only moving costs appear to play a quantitative role in such calculations.

(d) Subsidies are always positive. Spontaneous moves in undesirable directions are never taxed, although such a measure might aptly complement the subsidy system and reduce its net cost considerably.

(e) Last, but not least, our analyses took no regard at whether the individual was unemployed or not. The analysis accommodates the unemployed by taking account of unemployment payments. After worker migration the government derives an additional benefit from this factor which provides the opportunity of raising the subsidy. This benefit would relate to the estimated duration of the unemployment which would obtain if the individual were to act spontaneously. The analysis revealed, however, that from a macro-economic viewpoint, it makes little sense to limit assistance, if it is really needed, to the unemployed—though if it were limited the benefits might be even larger. However, if the stipulated conditions are fulfilled, assistance to anyone is justified, particularly when account is taken of the fact that subsidy levels should in principle vary with the individual's income gain and according to whether or not he would have received temporarily an unemployment payment.

These discrepancies between practice and principle are general in nature, and apply to all four countries. However, another factor is more appropriately considered on the basis of, on the one hand, France, and the Netherlands, and on the other, Sweden and Great Britain. The analysis set out in the first two sections can be applied generally to the former countries. In Sweden and Great Britain, however, the authorities are inclined not to 'correct' regional incomes, at least not in so far as migration policy is concerned, and therefore regard a move from the North to Stockholm or Göteborg or a move to the London area, just as desirable in the short run as any other move. This is a very significant difference. In the first two countries the subsidy is used to change a potential decision, to convert a spontaneous mover from $i$ to $j$ into an induced mover from $i$ to $k$. By this action a number of migrants who would have moved spontaneously will be subsidised, but, nevertheless, the subsidy is paid only if the migrant moves to a place where, at least in the government's view, spontaneous migration is inadequate. Since the developed regions are excluded from this group, most migrants are excluded from the subsidy too. In Sweden and Great Britain essentially any movement (of the unemployed) is subsidised; as a result, the number of subsidised moves in Sweden is many times greater than in the other countries. That the number of assisted moves in Great Britain is so low is probably attributable to poor publicity for the scheme.

It is not the purpose of this book to determine whether one policy is better than another. One important remark should be made however. Attention should be drawn to the enormous urban problems present in three of the countries when compared to Sweden. The major cities in these three countries (Paris, London and the Rimcity) display such serious signs of overurbanisation, traffic congestion, air pollution etc. when compared with those in Sweden, that it is not surprising that this contrast has an impact on both regional and migration policy. In this sense, it is quite understandable why these three countries deliberately choose not to subsidise migrants to such areas (or give little publicity to the fact that they do) whereas Sweden does. We shall not consider whether measures other than those affecting migration might limit the growth of the large cities more effectively.

It seems that there is yet another fundamental difference between conditions in Sweden and in the other countries. This difference can perhaps be explained from the deviating situation of Sweden sketched above. For it appears that in Sweden mobility is regarded as a virtue *per se*, whilst in the other three countries it is regarded with comparatively little enthusiasm.

So far our analyses have shown that high labour mobility is necessary for a successful migration policy, and it seems rather strange to propagate a migration policy but not the mobility of those supposed to move. Yet such an approach might result from apprehension that a mobile population would excerbate conditions in the conurbations, a fear that does not exist to the same extent in Sweden.

In our opinion there can be no support to the view that mobility is not a virtue in itself. Mobility stems from the ability to judge (and hence from education) and from the information used as a basis for judgement. It is difficult to maintain that the outcome of such desirable amenities would be anything but desirable itself.

Bearing in mind the relevant inter-country differences, it may nevertheless be concluded that the policy foundations in all four countries are not very firm. Although the policies have been implemented for a considerable period, no real effort has been made to strengthen their foundations or to evaluate carefully their impacts. Interesting and significant studies are in hand but it is not yet clear how their findings could influence current policies. Their scope may therefore be too restricted.

94

### 3.4 Country evaluation of actual policies

#### 3.4.1 General principles of evaluation

The policy evaluation will be based on two criteria: the *consistency* of the policy and its *efficiency*. A policy will be regarded as consistent if the various goals which it pursues are not in conflict with each other (that is, its *internal consistency*) nor with these of other policies (*external consistency*). The consistency of a policy is by no means automatic. Indeed some inconsistencies may be inevitable. An economic policy which simultaneously seeks to maximise growth, attain full employment, ensure a stable price level and secure equilibrium in the balance of payments would usually be internally inconsistent, since the pursuit of one of these goals precludes one, or more, of the others. In such a case, a compromise between the conflicting goals must be defined.

In this study, the phrases internal and external inconsistency are used in a rather narrow sense. A policy will be regarded as internally inconsistent if its explicitly established goals cannot be attained with any combination of instruments available. Consequently, external inconsistency between two policies exists if the combination of explicitly defined goals of both policies cannot be reached with any mixture of the instruments available for both policies together. A similar definition holds for more than two policies.

A policy will be called *efficient* if the instruments for its implementation are efficient. *Internal efficiency* is deemed to exist if the instruments contribute effectively to the policy's targets and *external efficiency* exists if these same instruments do not unfavourably affect the chances of attaining the targets of other policies.

Thus a policy is internally efficient in economic terms if the costs of using the instruments are less than the benefits created—measured as the contribution to target attainment. External efficiency exists if the costs of using the instruments do not give rise to lower net benefits from other policies. The concept of a policy efficiency is thus closely related to that of the policy's cost–benefit ratio.

A policy can be both inconsistent and efficient. The goals of such a policy would be amenable only to a limited attainment, though this is enough to justify the use of the instruments. A consistent but inefficient policy is one that displays an unfavourable cost–benefit ratio but is not characterised by conflicting goals.

In the following paragraphs an attempt has been made to adhere, as closely as possible, to this rather rigid framework. It emerges, however, that difficulties are encountered as a result of the vagueness of the definitions of objectives. Even so, there is purpose in retaining this approach since a conclusion that policy goals are inadequately defined is itself a form of policy evaluation.

### 3.4.2 The Netherlands

Prior to 1960 the *goals* of the Dutch migration policy were, essentially, to assist the unemployed to find jobs. In this period, migration to the Rimcity was also subsidised, but the regulations of 1960 ended this subsidy (except for handicapped workers) and thereafter migration policy was intended to serve the objectives of the regional (decentralisation) policy. The employment objective was retained, but only in the case of those who migrated to the development nuclei. A new provision was that key workers emigrating with their firm from the Rimcity to a development area could also be assisted financially.

Current goals differ little from these. The most significant change was introduced in 1965 when all workers above a certain skill level became eligible for a subsidy when migrating with the firm from the Rimcity. Since 1969, employees of manufacturing firms as well as service enterprises have been eligible.

To summarise, the goals of migration and regional policy are presented in summary form in Table 3.1.

It would seem that the goals established for the policy of assisting key workers to emigrate with their firms from the Rimcity, are identical with the regional policy objectives. As far as assistance to the unemployed is concerned, the immediate goal is to provide the structurally unemployed with an employment opportunity in a development area.

Table 3.1.

Goals of Dutch Migration and Regional Policy

| Goals | Migration policy | | Regional policy |
|---|---|---|---|
| | Assistance to unemployed | Assistance to key workers | |
| Balanced distribution of economic activity | . | × | × |
| Balanced distribution of population | . | × | × |
| Provision of employment for the structurally unemployed | × * | × | × |

* The Rimcity is an explicit exception.

96

Instruments in the migration policy consist solely of subsidies to eligible migrants. The regional policy provides a variety of subsidies to firms which move to a development area.

As far as policy consistency is concerned, the only possible problem is whether or not the objective of assistance to the unemployed moving to a development area conflicts with the goals of balanced population distribution and of economic activity—and vice versa.

The first question can be answered in the negative—with one caution, that the goal of providing work for the unemployed should be interpreted in a very narrow sense, namely *in as far as this employment is available in development areas*. This means that assistance to the unemployed is not itself a goal, but is completely subservient to the success of the regional— including key worker policy. Assistance to the unemployed in the form of job opportunities is given only in so far as workers are needed in the development areas, but in pursuing this goal the other goals are also served.

When the situation in Great Britain is evaluated, the basic relevant differences between the situation in the Netherlands and in Great Britain emerge quite clearly. In both countries there is heavy emphasis on regional policy, but in Great Britain, where this policy is insufficiently effective, the worker is helped to move to a job. In Holland he is not: it is assumed, *a priori*, that regional policy will be successful. The eventuality that it might not be, is not taken into account by migration policy.

The second question is, in fact, answered also. If the goals are reached and jobs created in development areas, then workers are needed to fill thcm. The subsidisation of movement to these places then supports the successful regional and key worker policies.

It is much more difficult to gauge the *efficiency* of Dutch migration policy. Private cost–benefit analyses have been initiated, but these need to be complemented by macro-economic cost–benefit analyses if the level of the subsidies and the efficiency of the policy is to be judged. The result of these calculations must be available before a final answer to this question can be given.

There is one point, however, that merits particular attention, for it is not quite clear why assistance to the unemployed is limited to those moving to development nuclei in development areas only, and why, more generally, the assistance is restricted to the unemployed.

Consider first the geographical restrictions. It is well known that development areas are essentially low income areas: they were before the war and they remain so. However, other areas—particularly those between the west, and the north and the east, together with those in the south-west—are developing satisfactorily. From the worker's point of view, therefore, a move to one of these areas, if not to the Rimcity, might be much more attractive than a move to the development areas. This implies that a smaller subsidy would suffice to induce a move to these areas with a continuously rising demand for labour. On the other hand, the subsidy needed to induce the migrant to redirect his move from one of these areas to a development area, would need to be considerable.

Plainly, the authorities prefer workers to move to the development areas but, as stated, work opportunities there are restricted by the very limited success of the regional and key worker programmes. It is also understandable that the government does not want to subsidise migration to over-urbanised areas. But it is not clear why reasonable assistance could not be available to the unemployed who are able to get a job in the intermediate areas. If the true policy goal is to help the unemployed then it should be taken seriously, and not pursued only in so far as it makes other policies successful. The government's preference for moves to development areas can always be expressed by larger subsidies for such moves.

It is interesting in this respect to recall the results of the statistical analysis which showed that the Dutch are mobile over shorter distances but almost as immobile as the French and the British over greater distances. This points to the need for a regional policy which, taking this factor into account, induces a stepwise development of the areas outside the Rimcity. Since the results indicated that the Dutch rank high in mobility for distances of about 100 km and low for distances of 300 km, a policy that aims firstly at a successful development of growth centres at a distance of about 100 km from the Rimcity and afterwards concentrates on the development of the periphery promises to be more rational and effective than one that seeks an immediate and large jump and disregards the fact that, at least as far as the supply-side of the labour market is concerned, areas so far away are beyond the average worker's horizon.

A second consideration relates to the fact that assistance is only given to structurally unemployed people, not to the employed. The prescription that specified moves—and thereby immigration into certain areas—will be subsidised, implies that emigration from certain other areas is promoted. If the emigrant is unemployed, the subsidy helps to solve the unemployment problem, in this area, directly. But our earlier analysis suggested that there may be a number of non-economic factors that, despite the subsidy, will induce the worker to remain locally and unemployed rather than take a job elsewhere. Now if an employed person could be induced to leave the area and the unemployed person moved into his job, the subsidy to the employed emigrant would have an appreciable secondary impact that contributes to the efficiency of migration policy.

That the subsidy is provided only for the unemployed raises another, even more general, question. In principle, the policy is intended to help the structurally unemployed to move to a job: in short, assistance is given to those who are in distress and are likely to remain so if they are not helped by the government. But the question which arises is: why should a similar subsidy not be made available to others who could also improve their position by moving, but, for some reason or another, are unable to meet the costs. There must be marginally employed or structurally underemployed people for whom such an equally cogent case for assistance could be made. It is worthwhile to consider this point in some detail carrying out the appropriate cost–benefit calculations in order to determine whether an extension of the eligibility criteria along these lines could enhance the efficiency of migration policy. The two points referred to above might yield a migration policy that is more efficient and more sound.

Little reference has so far been made to the provision of information as an element of mobility policy. We stated earlier that a successful mobility policy is a necessary condition for a successful migration policy, but in the Netherlands a rather different view is taken. There, it is claimed that greater mobility might result in moves which are undesirable from a national economic point of view. On the other hand, the desirable migration is limited by employment opportunities in the development areas. Consequently the government does not attach very high priority to the development of a mobile population and takes no specific measures to promote mobility.

Nevertheless, information about job opportunities in other areas is made available to anyone who visits the local Employment Office; and information about the accommodation and education etc., in the receiving areas is available at the Employment Office of that area—again, on request only. Furthermore, assistance in finding accommodation is not integrated into the programme but is left to the local authorities and estate agents. Nor are any plans for the reception and integration of the migrants systematically linked with the migration programme.

In fact all these factors suggest that mobility is not regarded as a virtue and that migration tends to be considered as a necessary evil by the central authorities—a process required for the sake of a successful regional policy or, at the most, for balancing geographical labour surpluses and deficits.

Such attitudes merit further and fuller consideration. The scope of the Dutch programme appears to be too narrow to provide effective support for such other goals of economic and social policy as growth, flexibility in the labour market and full and stable employment. Regional objectives should really not be the only goals of such an important element of labour policy. Further consideration of the proper goals of migration policy might broaden the schemes considerably and also contribute to higher and more stable employment and to the well-being of employed as a result of the improved structural adjustment of labour supply and demand.

### 3.4.3   Great Britain

The *general objectives* of British migration policy have remained unchanged since the war. The Key Workers' Scheme and the Nucleus Labour Force Scheme support the government's regional development policy by helping industry to move into development (or other assisted) areas. Through the medium of the Resettlement and, later, the Resettlement Transfer Scheme, migration policy supplements regional development policy by, in the short term, assisting those who have poor employment prospects locally to move to jobs in other areas. Changes in the precise coverage of the schemes and in their eligibility criteria have been carried out within the framework of the original legislation, so that the schemes may be evaluated in terms of their original objectives.

It follows that British migration policy is intended to support regional policy although not to the same extent as in the Netherlands (and moves to congested areas are subsidised, if eligibility criteria are fulfilled). This conclusion was reached in earlier chapters. In this respect, the British situation differs little from that in the Netherlands and France, and a tabular summary of British migration and regional policies would be, with minor qualifications, identical to that for the Netherlands (Table 3.1). (Assistance is given in Britain to the unemployed moving to congested areas.)

Thus British migration policy would appear to be internally consistent, but externally inconsistent in that regional policy seeks to retard growth in congested areas in favour of progress in the development (or intermediate) areas.

This inconsistency aspect merits further attention. The aims of regional and migration policy in Great Britain are: to promote a more balanced geographical distribution of economic activity; and to attain a higher level of employment. This second target is sought by migration policy in two ways: subsidising migration to development and intermediate areas in order to meet labour requirements resulting from the promotion of employment in these areas; and subsidising migration to other areas (including the larger urban areas) to the extent that migration to non-development areas is needed to ensure overall employment.

British policy recognises that regional policy can be successful only in the long run and in consequence must be complemented by action to subsidise out-migration from backward areas in the short term. Thus British policy acknowledges an element in overall employment policy, completely lacking in the Netherlands: the time dimension. It is instructive to compare the two countries' policies in respect of their consistency. The Dutch policy appears consistent with respect to the established goals, but might be inconsistent in the short run if it is accepted that promoting overall employment should be a major objective of economic and social policy,

100

particularly in the short term. British policy is consistent in the short term, but inconsistent over the long term if, and to the extent that, regional policy meets with success in the long run.

As far as policy *efficiency* is concerned, although the number of persons assisted is not the sole criterion of success, the policy has had no great impact in this sense in Britain. No alternative efficiency indicator is available, since there have been no studies of the costs and benefits of either migration or regional policy, although certain qualitative evaluations of the latter have been made. It should be remembered, however, that mobility in Britain is relatively low and therefore that response to government measures may not be very large.

It should be stressed that an absence of evaluation is not a feature peculiar to migration policy. Governments seldom evaluate any of their policies. And, whilst this situation is improving, it will be a long time before adjustments to existing policies are based on analyses of their past success.

As in the other countries, migration assistance in Great Britain is limited (apart from help to key workers) to the unemployed. Although the Department of Employment and Productivity ensures that information about migration assistance, jobs and housing in other areas is available to all potential migrants, the programme is nevertheless very narrow and not very appropriate to a situation in which structural developments require adjustments in all sectors and regions. It is not a policy of assistance to workers, but of assistance to the unemployed. It is not a policy which tries to ensure that the right man gets the right job, but one which ensures that the right man gets a reasonably appropriate job.

Another consistency aspect concerns housing policy. In the United Kingdom under the transfer schemes, contributions towards the legal expenses of buying and/or selling property can be paid. The British Government provides no assistance by purchasing property itself, though the National Coal Board scheme provides some housing assistance for transferees. In general, local housing authorities supply information to migrants or prospective tenants about local authority accommodation, and owner/occupiers normally use estate agents. No central agency is responsible for providing assistance in connection with a change of accommodation, though local authorities have been asked by the central government to adopt more flexible procedures when allocating houses to newcomers.[5]

Clearly there is no explicit integration of migration and housing policy. It would seem, therefore, highly desirable—particularly when account is taken of the housing situation in some areas—that migration policy objectives should be reconsidered in the light of their consistency with housing policy objectives.

A worker in a declining area who owns his own house may or may not be willing to move to a growth area; but even if a house is available there, he will be deterred from moving by the knowledge that he will have great difficulty in selling his present home. Indeed, experience indicates that he will inevitably make a loss on the transfer [6]. The answer may be a Government Scheme to buy up such houses at some national regional valuation, for the scheme can hardly be left to local authorities who would understandably be reluctant to operate it [7].

The government schemes are not concerned with assimilation problems in the new area. However, the National Coal Board scheme is and it is known that some private firms take measures to assist transferees, or new entrants from other areas, to adjust to the new location.

It is apparent from the way in which migration policy is intended over the long term to serve the objectives of regional policy, that in the United Kingdom, too, mobility is not regarded as a virtue unless it operates in ways thought desirable by the central government. However, regional policy is concerned only with some very broad objectives—total employment and its geographical distribution—and pays little respect to the nature of the employment. This is crucial for migration policy, since the latter is little more than a servant of regional policy, being basically concerned with total numbers of people and hardly at all with the sectors in which they are employed, or their occupations. If regional objectives were only defined not simply in terms of population or labour size but also in terms of the numbers of workers required per region per sector and per occupation, then it would become obvious that even in congested areas surpluses in one occupation occur simultaneously with shortages in others.

A migration policy which sought to balance all these surpluses and deficits would contribute appreciably to a better geographical distribution of the various labour force groups without conflicting with the general overall objectives of regional policy.

This conclusion is elaborated in the recommendations of the final chapter. Suffice it to state at this stage that there is strong impression of undue influence of British regional policy on migration policy. This seems to have prevented the improvement and refinement of migration policy, and for this reason (leaving aside the key worker schemes) it has been of limited assistance to the unemployed rather than forming an essential part of labour market policy.

### 3.4.4 *France*

As indicated in Chapter 2, the structure of French migration and regional policies resembles that of the Netherlands. Regional policy is directed at decentralisation from the Paris area, and migration policy conforms to this goal by subsidising key workers who move with their firms from Paris, and also unemployed workers who take jobs in designated development areas outside the Paris region. The latter are given assistance if their unemployment is due to structural adjustments in their former firms and if no jobs are available in their locality.

Thus, the *goal* of French migration policy is as limited as that of the Dutch policy. It can be categorised as assisting the unemployed, to take jobs in other areas provided that no work is available locally and they do not choose the Paris region. The effect of the objective is little more than a limited contribution to a much broader goal: the attainment of an optimal distribution of workers between jobs and regions.

One might ask (as for the Netherlands) whether the exclusion, as a basic principle, of such a region as Paris, is consistent with this broadly defined objective. It is not simply a matter of the total numbers in the Paris region but also of the distribution of the capital's working population between the various education and skill levels in relation to existing and future needs. As long as regional policy is apparently unconcerned with this aspect, migration policy might be regarded as consistent with regional policy. But if it were recognised that the economy as a whole could benefit from simultaneously assisting certain people to leave the Paris region and certain others to move in, without major consequences for net migration to or from the region, the consistency no longer obtains. In this situation regional policy goals would conflict with those of migration policy, since the latter is supposed to further the mutual adjustment of regionally dispersed labour supplies and demands of all kinds.

On the other hand French regional policy, in which the *métropoles d'équilibre* play a very important role, seems to be considerably more realistic than regional policy in the Netherlands, for instance. For French regional policy seeks to bring about a balance in regional development by promoting the growth of a limited number of certain larger agglomerations already in possession of a firm infrastructure. Thus, although Paris is excluded from the programme, a number of other important cities are included. In the Netherlands all cities neither depressed nor in a depressed area are excluded.

As previously stated, the number of beneficiaries under the French migration schemes is very small. And as far as is known to the authors, no quantitative attempts have been made to evaluate the efficiency of the policy. That extremely small numbers of people benefit from the schemes suggests however that the scheme's *private* economic efficiency, for the individual worker at least, is low. Nothing is known about the policy's national economic efficiency except that on the basis of very general discussions, qualitative in nature, it is thought to be satisfactory.

It is generally recognised in France that a more general education, focusing on the provision of basic rather than specialised skills, could contribute more than anything else[8] to an equilibrium of supply and demand in the various (sectoral and regional) labour markets. But it is perhaps not fully appreciated that such an objective could introduce exactly what is currently missing from migration policy, the reduction of barriers to movement to *any* place—including Paris—if such movement is beneficial to the individual and to the economy. Admittedly, the adoption of a more basic and general education would reduce specific occupational shortages in the Paris region, but it would also be conducive to movements that are currently regarded as undesirable.

In both France and the Netherlands, the basic factor is really that social costs in the larger cities to which migration is not stimulated are not, or not sufficiently, charged to their inhabitants and in consequence there can be a considerable discrepancy between these costs and the level of local taxes. Usually movement to a larger city implies for a worker a number of advantages such as higher wages, more and better amenities, etc., together with a tax rate that is not much higher than or even identical to, that in other regions. Such measures as the exclusion of the Paris region from migration schemes fail to touch the heart of the problem. They do not make this region less attractive, they only make other areas rather less unattractive.

As long as this basic problem is untouched, the fundamental objective of labour market policy, to promote growth, minimising unemployment and maximising the adjustment of demand and supply in all sections of the labour market, will remain illusory. Migration flows will continue along the conventional paths in no way affected by migration policy measures. The statistical analyses of Chapter 1 revealed that migration patterns are determined by very general rules and (with the exception of Sweden) are uninfluenced by policy measures. If migration policy is to be taken seriously, one needs to recognise this fact to appreciate that actual patterns deviate fundamentally from the goals that have been set and to define some form of optimum situation to be aimed at in the longer or shorter term.

It is likely that a major reason for the lack of policy coordination, even in France, is the absence of a set of consistent goals for general economic, regional and labour market policies. Perhaps such a set cannot be defined as long as there is an absence of quantitative knowledge about the efficiency of the instruments provided in the various policies; and as long as the rigidities in existing institutional structures (for instance, in the tax structure) prevent the rational formulation of policies. But, if this is the case, all the more important objectives should be kept in mind, and secondary policies should not simply be aligned with the goals of the strongest policy if the latter are illusory and unrealistic.

The information provided by the French mobility policy is rudimentary. As stated, the worker (and his wife) is entitled to a reconnaissance visit to his now potential location if it is more than 100 km from his locality. Otherwise, apart from the general information provided by the labour exchange offices, no specific measures are taken to supply systematic information to a potential migrant. As in the United Kingdom and the Netherlands, housing policy in France does not seem to be integrated with migration policy. It is regarded as the concern of the local authorities, which are sometimes successful in their policies and sometimes (as in Paris) not.

This discussion would not be complete without reference to the French plans for converting the existing labour market policy into one that attempts to embrace the whole labour market and to serve the needs of each individual worker by enabling him to obtain the most suitable job. The report of the Services des Affaires Sociales shows very clearly that the social security system should be modified so that it enables the individual worker to take risks without losing his basic social rights. 'Il s'agit en outre, de passer d'un système de sécurité ancien lié au maintien dans un poste, une entreprise, une localité, à un système fondé sur des garanties transférables, qui soient suffisamment proches des individus pour qu'ils se sentent accompagnés par elles.'[9]

This clearly indicates a desire to endow the individual with as much 'mobility' as possible, so that he can make untrammelled decisions for improvements in his situation. Complementary to this, there needs to be a system that provides the individual with sufficient information about alternative occupations and conditions elsewhere. We return to this topic in Chapter 4. At this stage it is important to appreciate that in France 'mobility' is regarded as a precondition for the individual reaching optimal employment, given his abilities and skills; also, that an element that permits this freedom of choice is to be 'footloose' in so far as social security is concerned.

The report referred to above emphasises the desirability of promoting mobility in a general sense and in so doing is very refreshing in comparison with the rather unimaginative rules of the narrowly defined French migration policy. Of particular interest is the following statement:[9]

En outre, du fait de sa jeunesse, de son niveau de formation plus élevé aussi, ce nouvel apport de main-d'oeuvre acceptera plus facilement des changements de résidence, et des changements professionnels. L'observation du passé le montre, ces catégories de population sont les plus mobiles professionnellement et géographiquement. L'aptitude moyenne à la mobilité de la population active devrait par conséquent en être augmentée. Enfin l'adaptation aux besoins de l'économie devrait en principe être mieux assurée puisqu'un pourcentage important de la population active sera sorti récemment de l'appareil d'éducation. Encore faut-il que la formation donnée par celui-ci corresponde bien à ces besoins.

Thus in France there is an awareness of the intrinsic importance of mobility. It is hoped that these ideas will be reflected in the future form of migration and mobility policy, not only to make it more realistic but, above all, to enable it to make the maximum contribution to the fundamental objectives of a true labour market policy.

### 3.4.5 Sweden

The goals of Swedish assistance to migrants conform with the general objective of Swedish labour market policy, namely to promote full employment and economic growth. These goals were intended to be essentially *economic* goals. It was felt that full employment and economic growth should be the major targets of national policy and that migration policy should help in their attainment. It may be claimed that these goals are still operative, but an examination of the use of the available funds reveals that social goals are implicitly served by migration policy.

The difference between migration policy in Sweden and in the other three countries is, that, as previously remarked, it is not the servant of regional policy in Sweden but pursues more general goals. Swedish regional policy is currently in a transitional phase. Up to now it has been limited to the provision of financial and other assistance to firms locating in the north. However, a government committee recently proposed the imposition of a special levy on building investment in such over-expansive areas as the Stockholm region. The levy will take the form of a compulsory interest free loan from those who invest in certain categories of building in the region, refunded after five years. Refund may be accelerated if the resources are used for investment in development areas.

The goals of Swedish migration (and mobility) and regional policy are summarised in Table 3.2.

The question whether or not migration policy is internally consistent can be answered in the affirmative in so far as the goal of economic growth is compatible with that of a balanced distribution of economic activities. A considerable proportion of the financial assistance is given to people migrating to larger urban areas, including Stockholm, where there is an urgent need for workers of all kinds. If the fulfilment of these needs is regarded as a contribution to the balanced distribution of economic activities, then the policy is internally consistent, if not, then there could be a conflict between the two goals. Whether or not there would be depends on the definition of a balanced distribution of activities. If this is defined as the equal distribution

106

Table 3.2.

Goals of Swedish Migration and Regional Policy

| Goals | Migration policy | Regional policy |
|---|---|---|
| Full employment and economic growth | × | × |
| Balanced distribution of economic activities | × | × |

of population and employment among the various regions then the goals conflict. If it is defined as that situation where no areas have an excess supply of, or an excess demand for, labour, then the goals do not conflict.

A relevant consideration is how economic growth is measured. If it is measured simply by national income, then the current migration policy certainly contributes to economic growth. If, however, economic growth is defined as the growth of national income *corrected for social costs in larger urban areas* then, again, there might be inconsistency.

In its present form the regional policy has little meaning. However, if the levy referred to above were introduced, it would provide a counterpart of the subsidies given to industries in development areas and, as noted, could stimulate investment in the development areas. If this policy should prove successful, then whether or not the demand for and supply of labour in, say, the Stockholm region would be in equilibrium, depends on the relative levels of investment taxes and migration subsidies. Such an equilibrium could only be reached if migration subsidies were given solely to those for whom Stockholm has a job. Since this condition seems improbable given the general context of labour market policy, the external consistency of the labour market policy might be effected by regional policy measures in Stockholm.

Since there are no specific cost–benefit studies of migration in Sweden, it is difficult to assess the policy's internal efficiency. Currently, a working unit is examining this aspect at Umeå University but so far no significant results have emerged.

The external efficiency of the Swedish migration policy is likely to be relatively high. This conclusion is suggested by the contribution made by the policy towards labour market equilibrium in the northern part of the country—an objective also pursued, though with different instruments, by regional policy. Whether or not migration policy will support the objectives of future regional policy in the Stockholm region, remains to be seen. Sweden ranks high in terms of the provision of information to potential migrants. Information about jobs is contained in the *Labour Market Journal*, which lists all vacancies, describes the work requirements and gives information about the availability and nature of accommodation. Information about public assistance is provided by Employment Offices in cooperation with employers.

The presence of appointment officers, at County Labour Boards in receiving areas is a promising development. However, follow-up procedures, once a worker has entered the area, are inadequate: a check that the migrant fulfils the starting-grant conditions is not sufficient. Nor is the special assistance, given to workers willing to sell their houses in areas of origin, very effective in practice, since prices offered by the authorities are usually unattractive. House construction is determined by five-year programmes formulated by the Government and Parliament. Restricted construction quotas are determined for the fourth and fifth year of these programmes and allocated to specific expanding locations: the full programme is reserved for the first year and integrated with business cycle developments. Regional quotas within the framework of the programme are determined by the National Board of Housing together with the National Labour Market Board. The aim of this cooperation is to secure a distribution of housing construction that is consistent with labour market requirements. On the regional level, the distribution of housing quotas between municipalities is determined jointly by the County Government (the regional planning authority), the County Housing Board and the County Labour Board[11].

In summary, it would seem that the Swedish migration policy is not only part of a broader framework of labour market policy, but hitherto has also served much wider objectives than in the other three countries. Moreover, the facilities provided are superior to those in the other three countries. In general, the measures seem to be effective and serve the country's general social-economic goals, namely full employment and fast growth.

If Sweden were to follow the regional policies of other countries, a conflict might arise between the goals of the migration and regional policies in as far as the latter did not fulfil expectations. This could lead to the reconsideration of the targets of a balanced population distribution and employment, and of economic growth.

## Notes

[1] For an interesting application of a private economic cost-benefit approach, see Jenness, op. cit. In this, approach is calculated by 'merely aggregating the differential benefits of: the worker in his first job in the destination area;

the worker in subsequent jobs; the wife during the same time period; and other dependents during a calculated time period, subjecting these to the probability function for the worker moving autonomously and the aggregate estimate related to the mobility grant and overhead costs with the worker's move' (op. cit., p. 13). For reasons that will become apparent the present study uses a somewhat different theoretical approach.

[2] Or a household.

[3] We write this benefit with a prime since the government obtains the present value using the objective interest rate, while the individual will use his private, subjective, interest rate.

[4] In other words, to consider the decision to stay in $i$ or move to $j$.

[5] The activities of the Scottish Special Housing Association are also relevant in this context.

[6] See 'Housing and mobility', *Financial Times*, 25 April 1963.

[7] Frederic Meyers (ed), 'Area redevelopment policies in Britain and the countries of the Common Market'. United States Department of Commerce 1965: 'Regional policy in Great Britain' by Alan J. Odber, p. 369.

[8] Compare Rapport du Groupe d'Etudes à Long Terme. *Mobilité et Coûts de l'Adaptation*, Commissariat Général du Plan. Services des Affaires Sociales. Paris, February 1970.

[9] Op. cit. p. 23.

[10] Op. cit. p. 17.

[11] It was felt by the County Labour Board that the Göteborg Municipality was uncooperative in providing accommodation for in-migrant workers.

# 4 Recommendations

## 4.1 Introduction: general outline of policies

Economic development is a complicated process of growth and decline in sectors and regions. Industries flourishing today may be stagnating or declining tomorrow, and skills now heavily in demand, may be soon obsolete. Similarly, regions, booming whilst their economic structure is favourable, can become underdeveloped tomorrow. Coalmining and textiles are the classic examples of activities that originally brought prosperity to many regions but are now a cause of regional distress.

The more a region is economically specialised, the greater the danger of distress if the principal activity declines and the more difficult the problems of adjusting to a structure that promises growth for the region. Such features and processes have significant implications for the pattern of labour demand in the various regions. This pattern adjusts to sectoral developments and to developments within each sector. Labour supply needs to be adjusted to this demand pattern in such a way that maximum employment is attained and economic growth is ensured.

The adjustment of labour supply to labour demand is the basic task of a labour market policy. Let us examine the adjustment process more closely. Let $P$ be the $m \times n$ matrix—$m$ levels of skill and $n$ sectors—of the percentage distribution of skills required by the various sectors. Thus $P_{ij}$ (the element in the $i^{th}$ row and $j^{th}$ column of the matrix) represents the demand for labour of skill level $i$ by sector $j$, expressed as a percentage of total demand for labour by sector $j$. Write $D_S$ for the $n \times k$ matrix ($k$ regions) of the distribution of absolute number of workers in the various sectors in all regions. Then $PD_S = D_k$ represents the demand for workers of different skill levels per region.

If $S_k$ is the matrix of the supplies of skill levels per region, then $PD_S - S_k = D_k - S_k$ represents the net demand (positive or negative) for the different skills in all regions. In such a matrix, a row sum indicates the total excess demand or excess supply for the relevant skill level in the country as a whole, and a column sum the total excess demand or excess supply for labour in the region in question. This matrix should be the starting point for both a labour market and regional policy. Both policies should aim at the mutual adjustment of surpluses and deficits in the various cells of the matrix.

Let us examine this matrix more closely. If we consider a single row, that is the net demand (positive or negative) for a given skill level in the various regions, a large positive total for the row elements would indicate that the particular skill is in heavy demand. The minimum number of workers who need to be (re)trained for that skill, is at least equal to this net positive demand.

The distribution of shortages and surpluses over the elements in the row indicates how far workers with this skill are in excess supply or demand in the various regions. Thus they show how far excess supplies in some regions could meet excess demands in others, and what migration flows would be required to bring this redistribution about.

A column sum reveals the overall labour market balance for the region in question. The *distribution* of workers over the various skill levels as shown within each column, indicates how far the regional labour markets are in equilibrium with respect to the supply and demand of particular skills. Rapidly expanding regions might show a surplus demand in all cells, declining regions an excess supply. Such a situation would clearly indicate the need for in-migration and out-migration respectively, to restore the inter-regional balance. A regional policy that tries to divert economic activities from congested to development regions could help adjust overall excess supplies in some regions to overall excess demands in others.

The optimum way of adjusting the surpluses and shortages shown in the cells of the matrix could be determined by a non-linear programme in which the 'costs' of moving workers, of training or retraining workers and of diverting industry are taken into consideration: in all three cases costs would be a function of 'distance', either between regions or between skills.

The problem becomes more complicated when account is taken of the fact that it is not, as sketched here, a static problem, but a dynamic one—adjusting changes in supply demand over time. Regional policy seeks to influence the development of labour demand in each region, and migration and retraining policy try to adjust the volume and structure of labour supply.

An illustration of how such an analysis can be implemented, is found in a study of Puerto Rico.[1] Although this analysis was applied to Puerto Rico as a whole, the principle is the same, and only the regional dimension would need to be added. It appears from this study that the set of matrices—one for each year—that emerge should form the basis for both an active labour market policy and a regional policy. It reveals the size and nature of the problem that has to be solved by both policies simultaneously.

In order to obtain the required matrices, there is a need to: determine each sector's demand for workers of different skills and forecast the development of this demand; forecast the development of each sector and its probable regional distribution; and estimate the skill supplies in each region, given existing and future age distribution, and the participation in education, training and retraining programmes. Once provisional manpower budgets per region, sector and skill-level have been obtained in this manner, quantitative goals (presented as a set of matrices) need to be established. This requires an interdepartmental approach which cannot be implemented without knowledge of the instruments that are to be used and of their effectiveness.

Some impression of the effectiveness of various instruments can be obtained by the statistical analysis of the factors which have determined industrial and labour force movements in the past, together with cost–benefit analyses for migrants and industries. On the basis of these analyses the instruments can be selected according to their efficiency.

It is then possible to formulate sets of *potential goals* that are attainable given the instruments available and their efficiency. From these sets the 'best' set can be selected and policy designed accordingly.

## 4.2 Integration of policies

It appears, therefore, that a solution of the problem requires not only that the various policies be coordinated but also that they be fully integrated. Policies integration is in fact the only guarantee that policies are both internally and externally consistent. If research for the design of the integrated policy is of a high standard, it should also yield a highly efficient policy.

Certainly there is a tendency in the countries under consideration for the scope of labour market policy to be widened. In Sweden, social elements have been introduced, and in the other countries economic considerations play a more important role than they have in the past. But it cannot be said that in any of these countries it is generally appreciated that the various policies use different instruments, of which neither the internal nor the external efficiency is known. No quantitative goals are being pursued, and in so far as occasionally some, rather ambitious, objectives have been defined the practicability of their realisation has hardly been considered.

The authors appreciate that the integration of policies, hitherto belonging to the domain of different ministries, might not be easy. Historically, training and retraining have been the responsibility of the Ministries of Social Affairs and education of the Ministries of Education. Regional policy is implemented by Ministries of Economic Affairs or of Technology, migration policy by Ministries of Social Affairs and housing policy by the Ministry of Housing. Policies integration would require the kind of intensive liaison between these three ministries which as yet does not exist. But if it is realised that we are in fact faced by one large problem, affecting considerable proportions of activity in all three ministries, it seems logical that, on the basis of appropriate research, the government should establish targets for the integrated policy and then apportion the task of implementation between the ministries involved. This, at least, would guarantee that each ministry operates on the same principles and attempts to reach the same targets. Annual policy reviews, each of the affected ministries would, on the one hand, show how far the objectives have been attained and, on the other, ensure a reasonable degree of coordination between the ministries.

## 4.3 Scope of a labour market policy

Clearly the scope of labour market policy as described in the section 4.1 is much wider than that of existing policies. The objective of a labour market policy that is integrated into a framework of social-economic policy should be to promote the mutual adjustment of the supply and demand of labour by region and by skill. It is a policy that embraces, in principle, each worker and each industry. It aims to bring about the efficient use of all skills in those places where both the worker's and the nation's interest are best served.

The implementation of such a policy requires institutions that will promote the necessary adjustments. Effective and modern labour offices should inform any worker about the opportunities open to him in other regions and in other skills. Information concerning the workers available in different regions and their skill levels should be made available to firms. Job offers should be accompanied by complete information about all aspects of the vacancy, about housing, about employment opportunities for women in the region in question and about local amenities. Job requests should include full information about the worker's level, experience and age, and about the structure and size of his family. Such basic data should be fed into a central computer that is linked with local units in all regions. The information and service provided should be of the appropriate quality for the importance of the problem involved.[2]

Existing institutions differ greatly from these 'ideal' organisations. In many cases labour offices are located in old obsolete buildings, having a dreary nineteenth-century atmosphere in which the unemployed queue for jobs and their unemployment benefits. It is little wonder that private enterprise is beginning to serve as the intermediary between supply and demand for higher level jobs. However useful private firms may be in this role, they impede the centralisation of placement work with the result that complete information is available neither for those trying to improve their position nor for those trying to find the right worker.

If the respective governments would provide modern and attractive offices that offer their placement services to a wide range of workers—if necessary charging a fee according to the nature of the job and the applicant—they would perform a worthwhile task, not only on the fringes of the labour market, but for the market as a whole. If airlines and hotel chains are technically capable of a similar job, it should not be difficult for the central authorities.

It should be stressed that the authors do not regard the current work performed by labour offices for the unemployed as unimportant. On the contrary, in any re-organisation of labour market activities these functions will continue to be of outstanding importance. Nevertheless they can be seen to be marginal in the context of labour market operations as a whole. To improve the position of an employed worker, socially as well as economically might be just as important as providing an unemployed worker with a job.

One difficulty that might be encountered by the implementation of this kind of policy would be possible: resistance from employers against labour offices finding better jobs for their employees. Such a reaction would be extremely short-sighted, since in the longer term all would benefit from an optimum distribution of workers among jobs. Only the worst firms would fear a loss of workers if the latter were informed about opportunities elsewhere—and this is exactly what the more attractive firms would appreciate. Therefore too much weight should not be given to possible employer objections.

### 4.4 Objectives of migration policy

All this implies that there can be no specific migration policy target independent of the objectives of a much more general labour market policy. Its goals should be the same, and its particular tasks defined within the framework of the more general objectives of labour market (including regional) policy. These objectives need to be based on knowledge of the numbers in the individual cells of the kind of matrix referred to above, not only on the sums of its rows and columns. As an illustration: if in the Rotterdam area there is a net deficit of workers with low skills and a surplus of workers with high skills, migration policy should recognise this and operate accordingly. The general rule, in the Netherlands and in France, that no migration subsidy should be paid to migrants to congested urban areas is much too crude to allow for a smooth adjustment of labour supply and demand by skill and by region, especially when rules apply only to the unemployed.

The basic weaknesses of existing migration policies are that: they neglect the interests of the employed; apply very general principles (which may hold for one skill level but certainly not for others); use as instruments only financial subsidies; and ignore the wider, social, integration problems that arise. In one sense they are too crude and too general, and in another, too precise and too restricted. There is a clear need for both the generalisation and integration of migration policy and for the refinement of the instruments with which it is implemented. This study has drawn attention to the kind of generalisation and refinement that is needed.

114

## 4.5 Final remarks

The authors are well aware of the difficulties which will be encountered in attempts to implement these recommendations. Civil servants, especially those in Ministries of Social Affairs, are little versed in the use of socio-econometric models as policy bases and even less in the procedure of comparing policy goals and impacts; they might even be unaware of the existence of goals other than helping the unemployed. It seems vitally important, however, that such attitudes be changed and more scientific methods adopted in Ministries of Social Affairs. The Netherlands, which has something of a tradition of econometric planning, has made a start and it is hoped that it will be successful and adopted by other countries. It is an approach that will raise the efficiency of labour market policy in general and migration policy in particular. Such an improvement in efficiency is precisely what is required, not as an end in itself but as a means of promoting human happiness, the ultimate goal of any government policy.

## Notes

[1] Dr. Miguel Echenique, *Demand for Human Resources in Puerto Rico*, Proceedings of the Economic Planning Seminar of the Commonwealth of Puerto Rico, 1958, Regional Technical Aids Centre. International Co-operation Administration Mexico, 1960.

[2] The required information should be standardised, at least at a European level. The OECD would be a suitable organisation for undertaking this task.

# Appendix

Matrix of Inter-regional Migration

| Destination \ Origin | PAR | CHA | PIC | HNOR | CEN | BNOR | BOUR | NORD | LOR | ALS |
|---|---|---|---|---|---|---|---|---|---|---|
| PAR | | 27.1 | 47.2 | 35.4 | 59.9 | 43.8 | 33.0 | 48.8 | 25.7 | 10.2 |
| CHA | 23.5 | | 14.2 | .8 | 1.6 | 1.2 | 5.2 | 8.8 | 16.1 | 2.0 |
| PIC | 49.7 | 9.3 | | 10.2 | 2.9 | 2.6 | 2.2 | 26.6 | 3.3 | .6 |
| HNOR | 34.5 | 1.5 | 10.0 | | 4.7 | 11.9 | 2.0 | 8.0 | 2.8 | .7 |
| CEN | 78.9 | 4.0 | 4.3 | 5.4 | | 6.4 | 7.7 | 6.5 | 4.7 | 2.3 |
| BNOR | 32.3 | 1.5 | 3.3 | 10.1 | 3.9 | | .8 | 3.7 | 1.2 | .6 |
| BOUR | 30.3 | 9.8 | 2.3 | .7 | 7.7 | 1.3 | | 4.6 | 5.5 | 1.7 |
| NORD | 20.3 | 3.7 | 22.1 | 4.1 | 3.3 | 1.3 | 2.1 | | 6.4 | 1.8 |
| LOR | 14.8 | 16.9 | 3.3 | 1.9 | 3.0 | 2.0 | 3.5 | 6.6 | | 12.0 |
| ALS | 6.5 | 2.4 | .7 | .7 | 1.8 | 1.0 | 1.6 | 2.4 | 18.2 | |
| FRAC | 8.3 | 4.7 | .8 | .5 | 1.1 | .3 | 10.4 | 2.5 | 10.1 | 3.2 |
| LOIR | 40.4 | 2.3 | 1.9 | 4.6 | 12.0 | 11.0 | 2.0 | 3.9 | 3.0 | 1.0 |
| BRE | 47.2 | 1.6 | 1.6 | 6.0 | 6.1 | 11.8 | 1.8 | 2.8 | 3.1 | 1.4 |
| POIC | 24.4 | 2.3 | 1.5 | 1.9 | 10.7 | 2.1 | 1.4 | 2.3 | 2.4 | .8 |
| AQU | 43.5 | 3.4 | 3.1 | 2.5 | 6.4 | 2.3 | 2.3 | 6.7 | 5.0 | 2.0 |
| MIPY | 29.3 | 1.8 | 2.4 | 1.3 | 3.4 | 1.3 | 1.6 | 4.5 | 3.8 | 1.5 |
| LIM | 16.6 | .8 | .8 | 1.3 | 4.4 | 1.2 | .6 | 1.0 | .5 | .2 |
| RHOA | 40.6 | 6.2 | 5.5 | 3.9 | 7.0 | 2.6 | 26.1 | 12.7 | 10.7 | 4.0 |
| AUV | 12.7 | 1.3 | 1.4 | 1.0 | 5.3 | 1.1 | 4.8 | 2.0 | 1.6 | .7 |
| LANG | 24.8 | 2.4 | 1.8 | 1.9 | 1.8 | 1.4 | 2.8 | 4.2 | 4.4 | 2.2 |
| PROA[1] | 76.5 | 7.2 | 4.8 | 5.8 | 6.5 | 3.9 | 7.5 | 11.9 | 15.4 | 5.5 |
| Total | 655.1 | 110.2 | 133.0 | 100.0 | 153.5 | 110.5 | 119.4 | 170.5 | 143.9 | 54.4 |

[1] Including Corsica.

Source: Compiled from I.N.S.E.E., Survivants en 1968 des Migrations entre 1962

**Legend:**

| | | | | | |
|---|---|---|---|---|---|
| PAR | = Région Parisienne | CEN | = Centre | LOR | = Lorraine |
| CHA | = Champagne | BNOR | = Basse Normandie | ALS | = Alsace |
| PIC | = Picardie | BOUR | = Bourgogne | FRAC | = Franche-Comté |
| HNOR | = Hte Normandie | NORD | = Nord/Pas-de-Calais | LOIR | = Pays de la Loire |

ance 1962–8 (Migrants in Thousands)[1]

| RAC | LOIR | BRE | POIC | AQU | MIPY | LIM | RHOA | AUV | LANG | PROA[1]) | Total |
|---|---|---|---|---|---|---|---|---|---|---|---|
| .1 | 52.9 | 64.0 | 36.0 | 44.3 | 35.6 | 16.5 | 39.0 | 20.0 | 24.0 | 49.5 | 723.0 |
| .6 | 2.2 | 1.5 | 1.5 | 1.6 | 1.7 | .9 | 2.8 | .9 | 1.3 | 3.0 | 94.4 |
| .6 | 2.2 | 2.4 | 1.8 | 1.7 | 2.6 | .7 | 2.5 | 1.3 | 1.4 | 2.2 | 126.8 |
| .9 | 4.4 | 6.9 | 2.1 | 3.0 | 1.4 | .7 | 2.1 | .8 | 1.4 | 3.0 | 102.8 |
| .3 | 16.8 | 7.8 | 15.3 | 6.5 | 4.7 | 5.3 | 5.8 | 5.8 | 2.8 | 5.0 | 197.3 |
| .6 | 13.0 | 9.4 | 1.1 | 1.9 | 1.2 | .6 | 2.5 | .7 | .5 | 2.3 | 91.2 |
| .9 | 2.5 | 1.1 | 1.2 | 2.3 | 2.1 | .9 | 18.6 | 6.0 | 2.0 | 4.2 | 114.7 |
| .2 | 1.8 | 3.2 | 2.0 | 2.7 | 1.7 | .9 | 3.4 | 1.3 | 2.9 | 4.3 | 90.5 |
| .9 | 2.7 | 3.1 | 3.1 | 3.9 | 2.8 | .8 | 5.8 | 1.9 | 2.4 | 5.4 | 101.8 |
| .3 | 1.6 | 1.4 | 2.4 | 2.0 | 4.9 | .3 | 6.0 | 1.2 | 2.2 | 5.7 | 69.3 |
|  | .9 | .9 | 1.0 | 1.6 | .8 | .4 | 7.5 | .6 | 1.2 | 2.6 | 59.4 |
| .8 |  | 25.4 | 14.5 | 5.2 | 2.5 | 1.1 | 3.3 | 2.1 | 2.0 | 3.6 | 142.6 |
| .8 | 23.8 |  | 4.4 | 3.7 | 1.7 | .8 | 2.0 | 1.0 | 1.9 | 9.1 | 132.6 |
| .9 | 16.9 | 3.7 |  | 15.1 | 2.9 | 5.1 | 1.3 | 1.7 | 1.6 | 3.4 | 102.4 |
| .7 | 5.3 | 4.6 | 21.2 |  | 26.0 | 6.6 | 4.8 | 3.1 | 5.1 | 8.0 | 163.6 |
| .0 | 3.3 | 1.6 | 3.8 | 24.4 |  | 3.7 | 7.9 | 4.9 | 18.1 | 9.0 | 128.6 |
| .2 | 2.0 | .5 | 6.2 | 6.4 | 4.3 |  | 2.0 | 5.2 | .7 | 1.2 | 56.1 |
| .1 | 5.3 | 4.9 | 4.9 | 9.2 | 9.7 | 2.6 |  | 21.9 | 19.5 | 39.6 | 247.0 |
| .6 | 1.6 | .9 | 2.3 | 3.1 | 3.1 | 6.9 | 15.3 |  | 3.5 | 4.1 | 73.3 |
| .1 | 2.1 | 2.2 | 2.3 | 7.3 | 19.7 | 1.5 | 13.7 | 3.6 |  | 24.9 | 126.1 |
| .2 | 6.2 | 10.1 | 6.1 | 12.1 | 12.8 | 1.9 | 40.7 | 6.6 | 28.8 |  | 275.5 |
| .8 | 167.5 | 155.6 | 133.2 | 158.0 | 142.2 | 58.2 | 187.0 | 90.6 | 123.3 | 190.1 | 3,219.0 |

68, DIV 98/V, 1968 RF 1/20°, July 1969 (three mimeographed tables).

| | | | | |
|---|---|---|---|---|
| RE | = Bretagne | MIPY | = Midi Pyrénées | AUV | = Auvergne |
| IC | = Poitou Charentes | LIM | = Limousin | LANG | = Languedoc |
| QU | = Aquitaine | RHOA | = Rhône-Alpes | PROA | = Provence-Côte d'Azur |

Table 2

Matrix of Inter-regional Migration in **Great Britain** 1961–6 (Migrants in Thousands)

| Origin / Destination | Northern | Yorkshire and Humberside + East/Midland | North Western | West Midland | East Anglia + South Eastern | South Western | Wales | Scotland | Total |
|---|---|---|---|---|---|---|---|---|---|
| Northern | | 36.9 | 15.9 | 7.3 | 30.2 | 6.9 | 3.0 | 14.3 | 114.5 |
| Yorkshire and Humberside + East Midland | 50.7 | | 49.5 | 39.9 | 112.3 | 20.1 | 10.2 | 33.1 | 315.8 |
| North Western | 18.6 | 47.6 | | 28.1 | 63.5 | 11.8 | 16.6 | 20.3 | 206.5 |
| West Midland | 18.5 | 36.2 | 26.1 | | 60.9 | 19.9 | 19.4 | 15.9 | 196.9 |
| East Anglia + South Eastern | 49.8 | 117.8 | 77.7 | 74.0 | | 119.6 | 38.2 | 65.5 | 542.6 |
| South Western | 9.5 | 27.1 | 20.2 | 37.7 | 173.4 | | 19.1 | 11.7 | 298.7 |
| Wales | 4.4 | 10.7 | 25.7 | 18.6 | 33.7 | 12.6 | | 4.4 | 110.1 |
| Scotland | 11.4 | 12.5 | 9.5 | 7.3 | 36.0 | 6.8 | 3.0 | | 86.5 |
| Total | 162.9 | 288.8 | 224.6 | 212.9 | 510.0 | 197.7 | 109.5 | 165.2 | 1,871.6 |

Source: Compiled from Census 1966, Table 2B, Migrants within five years preceding Census by area of former usual residence and sex.

Table 3

Matrix of Inter-regional Migration in the **Netherlands** 1961–6 (Migrants in Thousands)

| Origin / Destination | Gronin-gen | Fries-land | Drenthe | Overijsel | Gelder-land | Utrecht | Noord-Holland | Zuid-Holland | Zeeland | Noord-Brabant | Limburg | Total |
|---|---|---|---|---|---|---|---|---|---|---|---|---|
| Groningen | | 13.3 | 18.6 | 7.8 | 7.4 | 3.7 | 10.1 | 11.1 | 0.7 | 2.3 | 1.6 | 76.6 |
| Friesland | 10.6 | | 5.3 | 7.8 | 6.2 | 4.1 | 13.1 | 9.1 | 0.6 | 1.9 | 0.9 | 59.6 |
| Drenthe | 19.4 | 6.8 | | 11.2 | 6.2 | 3.3 | 8.1 | 8.9 | 0.5 | 1.8 | 0.9 | 67.1 |
| Overijsel | 7.7 | 9.2 | 10.5 | | 30.7 | 8.5 | 17.7 | 17.3 | 1.3 | 7.3 | 3.4 | 113.6 |
| Gelderland | 8.7 | 8.7 | 7.3 | 33.5 | | 31.3 | 39.7 | 50.8 | 3.5 | 30.3 | 14.3 | 228.1 |
| Utrecht | 4.3 | 4.6 | 3.2 | 8.8 | 28.2 | | 44.7 | 39.7 | 2.4 | 11.2 | 6.3 | 153.4 |
| Noord-Holland | 12.0 | 14.9 | 6.9 | 17.1 | 32.1 | 37.1 | | 78.3 | 6.2 | 21.5 | 11.0 | 237.1 |
| Zuid-Holland | 10.8 | 8.9 | 7.1 | 16.1 | 39.8 | 36.0 | 78.6 | | 12.6 | 35.9 | 12.3 | 258.1 |
| Zeeland | 0.6 | 0.5 | 0.5 | 1.2 | 2.6 | 2.1 | 6.3 | 10.3 | | 7.6 | 1.0 | 32.7 |
| Noord-Brabant | 2.5 | 2.5 | 2.0 | 8.2 | 30.5 | 13.8 | 26.8 | 45.2 | 9.7 | | 29.4 | 170.6 |
| Limburg | 1.1 | 7.0 | 0.8 | 3.6 | 13.6 | 5.4 | 11.3 | 14.6 | 1.2 | 27.1 | | 85.7 |
| Total | 77.7 | 76.4 | 62.2 | 115.3 | 197.3 | 145.3 | 256.4 | 285.3 | 38.7 | 146.9 | 81.1 | 1,482.6 |

Source: Compiled from Centraal Bureau voor de Statistiek, Statistiek van de Binnenlandse Migratie 1960–1961, 1962–1963, 1964–1965. Maandstatistiek van de Bevolking en Volksgezondheid, September 1967:300.

119

# Matrix of Inter-regional Migration

| Destination \ Origin | STOCK | UPPS | SÖDM | ÖSTG | JÖNK | KRON | KALM | BLEK | KRIST | MALM | HAL |
|---|---|---|---|---|---|---|---|---|---|---|---|
| STOCK |  | 14.3 | 16.0 | 11.7 | 6.1 | 2.4 | 6.5 | 4.0 | 3.4 | 10.8 | 1.9 |
| UPPS | 14.7 |  | 2.3 | 1.7 | .8 | .3 | .8 | .3 | .5 | 1.1 | .3 |
| SÖDM | 12.7 | 2.0 |  | 5.1 | 1.4 | .5 | 1.6 | .6 | .6 | 1.3 | 4.7 |
| ÖSTG | 8.9 | 1.4 | 4.8 |  | 4.9 | 1.0 | 5.7 | .9 | 1.0 | 2.3 | .6 |
| JÖNK | 4.9 | .7 | 1.3 | 5.3 |  | 3.9 | 4.3 | 1.1 | 1.3 | 2.8 | 1.7 |
| KRON | 2.4 | .3 | .6 | 1.1 | 4.6 |  | 3.7 | 2.3 | 2.6 | 3.1 | 1.1 |
| KALM | 4.8 | .6 | 1.3 | 4.5 | 3.5 | 3.3 |  | 2.1 | 1.0 | 2.1 | .4 |
| BLEK | 3.2 | .2 | .4 | .9 | 1.0 | 2.4 | 2.4 |  | 3.6 | 3.5 | .4 |
| KRIST | 3.4 | .6 | .7 | 1.2 | 1.4 | 2.9 | 1.2 | 3.5 |  | 19.3 | 1.9 |
| MALM | 14.1 | 1.4 | 2.0 | 3.8 | 4.3 | 4.1 | 3.6 | 4.5 | 22.7 |  | 3.5 |
| HALL | 1.9 | .3 | .5 | .6 | 2.0 | 1.4 | .6 | .4 | 1.8 | 2.8 |  |
| GÖTEB | 10.6 | 1.2 | 1.8 | 3.5 | 4.4 | 1.4 | 1.8 | 1.5 | 1.6 | 5.8 | 5.9 |
| ÄLV | 3.7 | .7 | 1.2 | 1.7 | 3.0 | .9 | 1.0 | .7 | .8 | 2.2 | 2.5 |
| SKAR | 3.3 | .7 | 1.1 | 1.4 | 3.2 | .7 | .8 | .4 | .8 | 1.3 | .7 |
| VÄRM | 4.5 | .8 | 1.3 | 1.0 | .8 | .3 | .5 | .2 | .4 | 1.0 | .4 |
| ÖRE | 5.8 | 1.2 | 3.2 | 3.3 | 1.3 | .4 | .7 | .4 | .4 | 1.3 | .4 |
| VÄSTM | 8.1 | 4.1 | 4.6 | 2.5 | 1.2 | .5 | 1.0 | .5 | .6 | 1.4 | .4 |
| KOPP | 7.7 | 1.8 | 1.7 | 1.1 | .6 | .3 | .5 | .3 | .3 | .8 | .2 |
| GÄVL | 8.1 | 3.9 | 1.3 | 1.0 | .5 | .2 | .4 | .3 | .3 | .7 | .3 |
| VÄSTN | 7.7 | 1.4 | 1.0 | .8 | .5 | .3 | .4 | .3 | .3 | .9 | .2 |
| JÄMT | 3.6 | .6 | .4 | .4 | .2 | .1 | .1 | .1 | .2 | .3 | .1 |
| VÄSTB | 5.2 | 1.3 | .7 | .6 | .4 | .2 | .3 | .2 | .3 | .9 | .2 |
| NORRB | 6.1 | 1.2 | .9 | .8 | .5 | .3 | .4 | .2 | .4 | .9 | .2 |
| Total | 145.4 | 40.7 | 49.1 | 54.0 | 46.6 | 27.8 | 38.3 | 24.8 | 44.9 | 66.6 | 28.0 |

Source: Compiled from Den Inrikes Omflyttningen Mellan Länen 1961–6

**Legend:**

| | | |
|---|---|---|
| STOCK = Stockholm | JÖNK = Jönköping | KRIST = Kristianstad |
| UPPS = Uppsala | KRON = Kronoberg | MALM = Malmö |
| SÖDM = Södermanland | KALM = Kalmar | HALL = Halland |
| ÖSTG = Östergötland | BLEK = Blekinge | GÖTEB = Göteborg och Bohus |

# veden 1961–6 (Migrants in Thousands)

| TEB | ÄLV | SKAR | VÄRM | ÖRE | VÄSTM | KOPP | GÄVL | VÄSTN | JÄMT | VÄSTB | NORRB | Total |
|---|---|---|---|---|---|---|---|---|---|---|---|---|
| | 4.8 | 4.4 | 6.8 | 8.3 | 11.4 | 13.4 | 14.1 | 15.9 | 8.6 | 9.7 | 12.5 | 197.8 |
| | .8 | .7 | 1.3 | 1.6 | 5.4 | 3.2 | 5.2 | 2.7 | 1.2 | 1.9 | 2.3 | 50.1 |
| | 1.1 | 1.3 | 1.9 | 3.5 | 4.9 | 2.7 | 1.9 | 1.9 | 1.3 | 1.6 | 2.2 | 56.1 |
| | 1.7 | 1.4 | 1.5 | 3.2 | 2.6 | 1.6 | 1.3 | 1.3 | .8 | 1.2 | 1.7 | 52.1 |
| | 3.5 | 3.7 | 1.0 | 1.3 | 1.2 | 1.1 | .7 | .7 | .4 | .6 | 1.0 | 45.2 |
| | .9 | .6 | .4 | .5 | .7 | .4 | .3 | .4 | .2 | .5 | .7 | 28.5 |
| | .9 | .6 | .6 | .8 | .8 | .5 | .5 | .6 | .2 | .4 | .5 | 31.1 |
| | .7 | .5 | .4 | .5 | .6 | .4 | .4 | .5 | .2 | .3 | .5 | 24.1 |
| | 1.1 | .8 | .7 | .7 | .7 | .5 | .5 | .5 | .3 | .7 | .7 | 44.9 |
| | 3.1 | 1.8 | 1.5 | 2.2 | 2.2 | 1.6 | 1.4 | 1.8 | .7 | 1.3 | 1.6 | 89.3 |
| | 3.5 | 1.0 | .6 | .6 | .6 | .4 | .3 | .4 | .2 | .4 | .4 | 29.3 |
| | 20.7 | 6.0 | 5.3 | 3.5 | 2.0 | 2.3 | 1.6 | 2.0 | 1.0 | 1.4 | 1.9 | 87.2 |
| | | 6.2 | 4.2 | 1.7 | 1.2 | 1.3 | .9 | 1.1 | .5 | 1.0 | 1.5 | 58.8 |
| | 6.3 | | 2.2 | 2.4 | 1.1 | .9 | .7 | .8 | .5 | .6 | 1.0 | 35.1 |
| | 3.6 | 1.7 | | 4.5 | 1.7 | 2.8 | 1.1 | .9 | .7 | .8 | .9 | 33.1 |
| | 1.6 | 2.7 | 6.5 | | 4.4 | 4.1 | 1.5 | 1.5 | .8 | 1.1 | 1.2 | 45.9 |
| | 1.4 | 1.1 | 2.4 | 5.3 | | 7.4 | 3.4 | 2.6 | 2.0 | 2.3 | 3.0 | 57.4 |
| | .9 | .7 | 2.8 | 3.4 | 5.7 | | 5.1 | 1.9 | 1.8 | 1.4 | 1.6 | 41.9 |
| | .8 | .5 | 1.2 | 1.2 | 2.8 | 5.7 | | 5.5 | 2.9 | 2.1 | 2.1 | 42.8 |
| | .7 | .6 | .8 | .8 | 1.6 | 1.7 | 4.7 | | 4.9 | 6.3 | 3.2 | 40.2 |
| | .3 | .2 | .4 | .4 | .9 | 1.3 | 1.8 | 4.2 | | 1.6 | 1.0 | 18.7 |
| | .5 | .4 | .6 | .6 | 1.1 | 1.1 | 1.3 | 5.1 | 1.4 | | 6.4 | 29.7 |
| | .7 | .5 | .6 | .8 | 1.4 | 1.1 | 1.4 | 2.3 | .9 | 6.6 | | 29.3 |
| | 59.6 | 37.4 | 43.7 | 47.8 | 55.0 | 55.5 | 50.1 | 54.6 | 31.5 | 43.8 | 47.9 | 1,168.6 |

| | | |
|---|---|---|
| .V = Älvsborg | VÄSTM = Västmanland | JÄMT = Jämtland |
| AR = Skaraborg | KOPP = Kopparberg | VÄSTB = Västerbotten |
| RM = Värmland | GÄVL = Gävleborg | NORR = Norrbotten |
| RE = Örebro | VÄSTN = Västernorrland | |

Table 5

Regional Employment[1] and Labour Force[2] in **France** and **Great Britain**

| France | | | Great Britain | | |
|---|---|---|---|---|---|
| Region[3] | Employment 1962 in 1,000s[4] | Labour Force 1962 in 1,000s[5] | Region | Employment 1960 in 1,000s[6] | Labour Force 1960 in 1,000s[7] |
| PAR | 3,893.8 | 5,776.9 | Northern | 1,231.1 | 2,098.0 |
| CHA | 371.7 | 726.6 | Yorkshire and Humberside + East Midland | 3,283.3 | 5,072.0 |
| PIC | 444.5 | 880.8 | North Western | 2,917.8 | 4,271.0 |
| HNOR | 462.2 | 855.2 | West Midland | 2,163.7 | 3,085.0 |
| CEN | 553.7 | 1,130.0 | East Anglia + South Eastern | 7,711.9 | 11,431.0 |
| BNOR | 307.0 | 730.3 | South Western | 1,155.1 | 2,154.0 |
| BOUR | 414.3 | 868.4 | Wales | 920.9 | 1,714.0 |
| NORD | 1,183.8 | 2,225.6 | Scotland | 2,000.0 | 3,377.5 |
| LOR | 744.1 | 1,365.9 | | | |
| ALS | 456.4 | 835.2 | | | |
| FRAC | 295.9 | 581.4 | | | |
| LOIR | 644.4 | 1,479.4 | | | |
| BRE | 574.4 | 1,493.1 | | | |
| POIC | 356.5 | 876.6 | | | |
| AQU | 645.7 | 1,463.1 | | | |
| MIPY | 515.8 | 1,336.8 | | | |
| LIM | 180.0 | 459.1 | | | |
| RHOA | 1,415.5 | 2,617.5 | | | |
| AUV | 335.0 | 794.7 | | | |
| LANG | 374.6 | 1,021.0 | | | |
| PROA | 982.3 | 1,932.7 | | | |

[1] Non-agricultural jobs only.
[2] People aged 15–64.
[3] For full names see Table 1.
[4] Compiled from Rapport Général de la Commission de la Main d'Oeuvre, op. cit.: 234, 243.
[5] Compiled from I.N.S.E.E., Etudes et Conjonctures. L'Espace Economique Français, Fascicule I, Démographie Générale, Paris 1965: 102–103.
[6] Compiled from data provided by the Department of Employment and Productivity.
[7] Compiled from General Register Office, The Registrar General's Statistical Review of England and Wales for the year 1960, Part II, Tables Population, London 1962.

# Table 6

## Regional Employment[1] and Labour Force[2] in Sweden and in the Netherlands

### Sweden

| Region[3] | Employment 1960 in thousands[4] | Labour Force 1960 in thousands[5] |
|---|---|---|
| STOCK | 585.4 | 866.4 |
| UPPS | 58.7 | 108.7 |
| SÖDM | 83.5 | 148.4 |
| OSTG | 130.2 | 234.7 |
| JÖNK | 102.5 | 186.2 |
| KRON | 50.6 | 102.2 |
| KALM | 74.6 | 153.1 |
| BLEK | 49.9 | 94.5 |
| KRIST | 82.7 | 164.4 |
| MALM | 254.4 | 416.2 |
| HALL | 55.4 | 110.3 |
| GÖTEB | 257.8 | 419.8 |
| ÄLV | 144.4 | 246.9 |
| SKAR | 78.6 | 160.6 |
| VÄRM | 97.6 | 192.2 |
| ÖRE | 99.6 | 174.0 |
| VÄSTM | 89.1 | 153.4 |
| KOPP | 99.3 | 185.9 |
| GAVL | 100.8 | 192.1 |
| VÄSTN | 96.4 | 187.9 |
| JÄMT | 38.8 | 89.8 |
| VÄSTB | 69.9 | 157.5 |
| NORRB | 82.3 | 170.0 |

### Netherlands

| Region | Employment 1960 in thousands[6] | Labour Force 1960 in thousands[7] |
|---|---|---|
| Groningen | 136.8 | 295.2 |
| Friesland | 117.2 | 281.9 |
| Drenthe | 73.6 | 188.6 |
| Overijssel | 243.0 | 488.1 |
| Gelderland | 357.8 | 773.0 |
| Utrecht | 210.7 | 416.5 |
| Noord-Holland | 691.3 | 1,291.7 |
| Zuid-Holland | 883.6 | 1,688.5 |
| Zeeland | 71.8 | 172.1 |
| Noord-Brabant | 453.7 | 905.3 |
| Limburg | 268.2 | 539.5 |

[1] Non-agricultural jobs only.
[2] People aged 15–64.
[3] For full names see Table 4.
[4] Compiled from data provided by the Arbetsmarknadsstyrelsen.
[5] Compiled from Statistik Årsbok för Sverige 1963: 22–23.
[6] Compiled from C.B.S., Arbeidsvolume en Geregistreerde Arbeids-reserve.
[7] Compiled from C.B.S., Jaarcijfers voor Nederland 1961–1962.

Table 7

Inter-regional Distances in **France** (in Automobile Kilometres)

| | 01 | 02 | 03 | 04 | 05 | 06 | 07 | 08 | 09 | 10 | 11 | 12 | 13 | 14 | 15 | 16 | 17 | 18 | 19 | 20 | 21 |
|---|---|---|---|---|---|---|---|---|---|---|---|---|---|---|---|---|---|---|---|---|---|
| 01 PAR[1] : Paris | — | 160 | 131 | 140 | 116 | 227 | 323 | 228 | 312 | 456 | 387 | 394 | 361 | 337 | 562 | 681 | 375 | 471 | 382 | 764 | 797 |
| 02 CHA : Chalons-s.-M | | — | 189 | 219 | 266 | 306 | 230 | 239 | 152 | 416 | 308 | 583 | 550 | 484 | 709 | 801 | 495 | 427 | 421 | 720 | 753 |
| 03 PIC : Amiens | | | — | 116 | 262 | 246 | 419 | 117 | 350 | 522 | 480 | 488 | 414 | 453 | 678 | 827 | 521 | 589 | 524 | 882 | 915 |
| 04 HNOR: Rouen | | | | — | 199 | 130 | 454 | 226 | 414 | 586 | 527 | 372 | 298 | 377 | 602 | 764 | 458 | 611 | 498 | 904 | 937 |
| 05 CEN : Orléans | | | | | — | 261 | 288 | 379 | 396 | 524 | 382 | 317 | 284 | 218 | 443 | 565 | 259 | 389 | 299 | 663 | 696 |
| 06 BNOR: Caen | | | | | | — | 541 | 356 | 544 | 685 | 614 | 279 | 173 | 334 | 559 | 739 | 433 | 649 | 528 | 877 | 956 |
| 07 BOUR: Dijon | | | | | | | — | 475 | 249 | 312 | 94 | 593 | 572 | 433 | 637 | 664 | 401 | 197 | 280 | 490 | 523 |
| 08 NORD: Lille | | | | | | | | — | 354 | 551 | 509 | 598 | 524 | 570 | 795 | 944 | 638 | 672 | 617 | 965 | 998 |
| 09 LOR : Metz | | | | | | | | | — | 161 | 258 | 713 | 680 | 615 | 839 | 913 | 647 | 446 | 529 | 739 | 772 |
| 10 ALS : Strasbourg | | | | | | | | | | — | 226 | 841 | 808 | 742 | 967 | 974 | 695 | 434 | 574 | 727 | 760 |
| 11 FRAC : Besançon | | | | | | | | | | | — | 669 | 666 | 509 | 681 | 748 | 469 | 208 | 348 | 501 | 534 |
| 12 LOIR : Nantes | | | | | | | | | | | | — | 106 | 179 | 329 | 579 | 297 | 607 | 469 | 741 | 914 |
| 13 BRE : Rennes | | | | | | | | | | | | | — | 251 | 435 | 685 | 369 | 645 | 507 | 813 | 952 |
| 14 POIC : Poitiers | | | | | | | | | | | | | | — | 225 | 424 | 118 | 428 | 290 | 562 | 735 |
| 15 AQU : Bordeaux | | | | | | | | | | | | | | | — | 250 | 219 | 549 | 369 | 497 | 661 |
| 16 MIPY : Toulouse | | | | | | | | | | | | | | | | — | 306 | 540 | 389 | 247 | 411 |
| 17 LIM : Limoges | | | | | | | | | | | | | | | | | — | 364 | 184 | 444 | 620 |
| 18 RHOA : Lyon | | | | | | | | | | | | | | | | | | — | 180 | 293 | 326 |
| 19 AUV : Clermont-Ferrand | | | | | | | | | | | | | | | | | | | — | 367 | 466 |
| 20 LANG : Montpellier | | | | | | | | | | | | | | | | | | | | — | 164 |
| 21 PROA : Marseilles | | | | | | | | | | | | | | | | | | | | | — |

[1] Compare Table 1 for full names.

Source: Compiled from the Michelin maps 'France Sud' and 'France Nord'.

124

Table 8

Inter-regional Distances in **Great Britain** (in Automobile Kilometres)

| | 01 | 02 | 03 | 04 | 05 | 06 | 07 | 08 |
|---|---|---|---|---|---|---|---|---|
| 01 Northern: Newcastle upon Tyne | – | 189 | 206 | 323 | 441 | 459 | 481 | 171 |
| 02 Yorkshire Humberside+East Midlands: Leeds/Nottingham[1] | | – | 64 | 134 | 263 | 271 | 294 | 348 |
| 03 North Western: Manchester | | | – | 127 | 296 | 256 | 277 | 338 |
| 04 West Midlands: Birmingham | | | | – | 177 | 140 | 164 | 460 |
| 05 East Anglia+South Eastern: London | | | | | – | 287 | 248 | 600 |
| 06 South Western: Bristol | | | | | | – | 71 | 586 |
| 07 Wales: Cardiff | | | | | | | – | 592 |
| 08 Scotland: Edinburgh | | | | | | | | – |

[1] The point on the line Leeds-Nottingham resulting from weighting the distance with the population shares of Yorkshire and Humberside (8.7% of the British population and of the East Midlands (6.0%)).

Source: A. A. Members Handbook (converted from mileage table).

Table 9

Inter-regional Distances in the **Netherlands** (in Automobile Kilometres)

| | 01 | 02 | 03 | 04 | 05 | 06 | 07 | 08 | 09 | 10 | 11 |
|---|---|---|---|---|---|---|---|---|---|---|---|
| 01 Gr[1] : Groningen | – | 58 | 28 | 147 | 164 | 190 | 198 | 246 | 361 | 247 | 321 |
| 01 Fr : Leeuwarden | | – | 73 | 163 | 160 | 186 | 135 | 210 | 357 | 243 | 317 |
| 03 Dr : Assen | | | – | 114 | 136 | 162 | 187 | 218 | 333 | 219 | 293 |
| 04 Ov : Enschede | | | | – | 84 | 136 | 160 | 196 | 298 | 167 | 241 |
| 05 G : Arnhem | | | | | – | 63 | 101 | 111 | 214 | 83 | 157 |
| 06 U : Utrecht | | | | | | – | 38 | 55 | 170 | 86 | 179 |
| 07 N.H.: Amsterdam | | | | | | | – | 72 | 181 | 121 | 214 |
| 08 Z.H.: Rotterdam | | | | | | | | – | 111 | 114 | 202 |
| 09 Z. : Middelburg | | | | | | | | | – | 159 | 247 |
| 10 N.B.: Eindhoven | | | | | | | | | | – | 90 |
| 11 L : Maastricht | | | | | | | | | | | – |

[1] Compare Table 3.
Source: The ANWB automap of the Netherlands

## Table 10
### Inter-regional Distances in **Sweden** (in Automobile Kilometres)

| | 01 | 02 | 03 | 04 | 05 | 06 | 07 | 08 | 09 | 10 | 11 | 12 | 13 | 14 | 15 | 16 | 17 | 18 | 19 | 20 | 21 | 22 | 23 |
|---|---|---|---|---|---|---|---|---|---|---|---|---|---|---|---|---|---|---|---|---|---|---|---|
| 01 STOCK[1] : Stockholm | — | 72 | 110 | 165 | 332 | 455 | 444 | 559 | 562 | 625 | 502 | 493 | 423 | 340 | 310 | 192 | 115 | 245 | 182 | 418 | 572 | 707 | 990 |
| 02 UPPS : Uppsala | | — | 111 | 237 | 381 | 504 | 516 | 608 | 611 | 674 | 551 | 474 | 431 | 321 | 291 | 173 | 81 | 169 | 110 | 346 | 500 | 635 | 918 |
| 03 SÖDM : Eskilstuna | | | — | 111 | 278 | 401 | 390 | 505 | 508 | 571 | 448 | 383 | 340 | 230 | 200 | 82 | 45 | 204 | 199 | 435 | 558 | 724 | 1,007 |
| 04 ÖSTG : Norrköping | | | | — | 167 | 290 | 275 | 394 | 397 | 460 | 337 | 329 | 258 | 216 | 231 | 118 | 150 | 305 | 347 | 583 | 690 | 872 | 1,155 |
| 05 JÖNK : Jönköping | | | | | — | 123 | 233 | 227 | 230 | 293 | 170 | 162 | 91 | 89 | 256 | 208 | 300 | 400 | 454 | 690 | 785 | 979 | 1,269 |
| 06 KRON : Växjö | | | | | | — | 110 | 104 | 136 | 209 | 140 | 287 | 214 | 212 | 379 | 331 | 423 | 523 | 577 | 813 | 908 | 1,102 | 1,385 |
| 07 KALM : Kalmar | | | | | | | — | 89 | 205 | 303 | 250 | 397 | 324 | 322 | 489 | 377 | 527 | 569 | 626 | 862 | 954 | 1,151 | 1,434 |
| 08 BLEK : Karlskrona | | | | | | | | — | 124 | 222 | 244 | 391 | 318 | 316 | 483 | 435 | 530 | 627 | 681 | 917 | 1,012 | 1,206 | 1,489 |
| 09 KRIST : Kristianstad | | | | | | | | | — | 98 | 125 | 272 | 287 | 319 | 486 | 438 | 593 | 630 | 684 | 920 | 1,105 | 1,209 | 1,492 |
| 10 MALM : Malmö | | | | | | | | | | — | 133 | 280 | 295 | 382 | 537 | 501 | | 693 | 747 | 983 | 1,078 | 1,272 | 1,555 |
| 11 HALL : Halmstad | | | | | | | | | | | — | 147 | 162 | 234 | 404 | 378 | 470 | 570 | 624 | 860 | 955 | 1,149 | 1,432 |
| 12 GÖTEB : Göteborg | | | | | | | | | | | | — | 71 | 160 | 257 | 301 | 393 | 493 | 547 | 783 | 878 | 1,072 | 1,355 |
| 13 ÄLV : Borås | | | | | | | | | | | | | — | 110 | 274 | 258 | 350 | 450 | 504 | 740 | 835 | 1,029 | 1,312 |
| 14 SKAR : Skövde | | | | | | | | | | | | | | — | 167 | 148 | 240 | 340 | 394 | 630 | 725 | 919 | 1,202 |
| 15 VÄRM : Karlstad | | | | | | | | | | | | | | | — | 118 | 210 | 248 | 344 | 557 | 633 | 846 | 1,129 |
| 16 ÖRE : Örebro | | | | | | | | | | | | | | | | — | 92 | 192 | 246 | 482 | 577 | 771 | 1,054 |
| 17 VÄSTM : Västerås | | | | | | | | | | | | | | | | | — | 159 | 154 | 390 | 513 | 679 | 962 |
| 18 KOPP : Falun | | | | | | | | | | | | | | | | | | — | 96 | 309 | | 598 | 881 |
| 19 GÄVL : Gävle | | | | | | | | | | | | | | | | | | | — | 236 | 385 | 525 | 808 |
| 20 VÄSTN : Sundsvall | | | | | | | | | | | | | | | | | | | | — | 191 | 289 | 572 |
| 21 JÄMT : Östersund | | | | | | | | | | | | | | | | | | | | | — | 388 | 641 |
| 22 VÄSTB : Umeå | | | | | | | | | | | | | | | | | | | | | | — | 283 |
| 23 NORRB : Luleå | | | | | | | | | | | | | | | | | | | | | | | — |

[1] Compare Table 4.

Source: Compiled from data provided by the Arbetsmarknadsstyrelsen.

## Matrix of Subsidised Inter-regional Migration in Swed

| Destination \\ Origin | STOCK | UPPS | SÖDM | ÖSTG | JÖNK | KRON | KALM | BLEK | KRIST | MALM | HALL |
|---|---|---|---|---|---|---|---|---|---|---|---|
| STOCK¹ |  | 54 | 22 | 18 | 8 | 4 | 8 | 5 | 6 | 23 | 10 |
| UPPS | 277 |  | 60 | 28 | 20 | 8 | 21 | 4 | 13 | 22 | 7 |
| SÖDM | 309 | 27 |  | 86 | 35 | 16 | 13 | 10 | 6 | 36 | 5 |
| ÖSTG | 202 | 18 | 62 |  | 49 | 13 | 27 | 17 | 9 | 61 | 5 |
| JÖNK | 110 | 9 | 25 | 56 |  | 40 | 40 | 9 | 24 | 64 | 11 |
| KRON | 80 | 6 | 15 | 28 | 92 |  | 34 | 51 | 46 | 104 | 22 |
| KALM | 298 | 26 | 49 | 162 | 125 | 109 |  | 69 | 26 | 117 | 14 |
| BLEK | 115 | 10 | 20 | 31 | 43 | 86 | 67 |  | 63 | 158 | 7 |
| KRIST | 36 | 5 | 7 | 16 | 17 | 39 | 9 | 39 |  | 219 | 12 |
| MALM | 65 | 3 | 16 | 33 | 36 | 34 | 21 | 51 | 47 |  | 18 |
| HALL | 27 | 8 | 9 | 15 | 40 | 24 | 9 | 8 | 29 | 74 |  |
| GÖTEB | 118 | 4 | 24 | 29 | 39 | 30 | 23 | 11 | 9 | 39 | 35 |
| ÄLV | 94 | 15 | 19 | 24 | 49 | 30 | 14 | 12 | 9 | 55 | 51 |
| SKAR | 76 | 9 | 19 | 36 | 48 | 12 | 11 | 5 | 15 | 32 | 10 |
| VÄRM | 509 | 38 | 97 | 166 | 72 | 33 | 17 | 14 | 42 | 152 | 33 |
| ÖRE | 275 | 26 | 55 | 68 | 43 | 12 | 9 | 17 | 10 | 55 | 7 |
| VÄSTM | 338 | 89 | 90 | 42 | 31 | 19 | 11 | 4 | 14 | 41 | 11 |
| KOPP | 1,868 | 273 | 231 | 85 | 91 | 39 | 39 | 41 | 47 | 188 | 25 |
| GÄVL | 2,071 | 462 | 148 | 87 | 54 | 30 | 40 | 39 | 76 | 147 | 17 |
| VÄSTN | 3,179 | 324 | 231 | 166 | 124 | 67 | 106 | 101 | 59 | 340 | 59 |
| JÄMT | 2,409 | 164 | 264 | 171 | 76 | 66 | 36 | 23 | 35 | 138 | 32 |
| VÄSTB | 2,539 | 286 | 404 | 267 | 209 | 258 | 94 | 76 | 226 | 420 | 112 |
| NORRB | 4,489 | 469 | 642 | 496 | 313 | 217 | 172 | 226 | 160 | 593 | 91 |
| Total | 19,484 | 2,325 | 2,509 | 2,110 | 1,614 | 1,187 | 821 | 832 | 971 | 3,068 | 594 |

¹ Compare Table 4 for full names.

63–6 (Absolute Number of Beneficiaries from Starting Assistance)

| TEB | ÄLV | SKAR | VÄRM | ÖRE | VÄSTM | KOPP | GÄVL | VÄSTN | JÄMT | VÄSTB | NORRB | Total |
|---|---|---|---|---|---|---|---|---|---|---|---|---|
| 23 | 12 | 11 | 3 | 7 | 10 | 10 | 12 | 9 | 4 | 18 | 21 | 298 |
| 20 | 19 | 25 | 35 | 31 | 111 | 61 | 124 | 76 | 36 | 73 | 62 | 1,134 |
| 45 | 24 | 13 | 23 | 47 | 88 | 22 | 24 | 12 | 8 | 10 | 7 | 873 |
| 51 | 35 | 16 | 10 | 21 | 47 | 9 | 7 | 12 | 9 | 2 | 2 | 684 |
| 52 | 33 | 39 | 6 | 22 | 34 | 6 | 9 | 3 | 5 | 5 | 2 | 614 |
| 27 | 17 | 20 | 5 | 10 | 30 | 3 | 1 | 2 | 2 | 4 | 2 | 601 |
| 14 | 29 | 20 | 9 | 23 | 52 | 15 | 4 | 6 | 6 | 1 | 10 | 1,284 |
| 48 | 16 | 12 | 5 | 12 | 27 | 5 | 4 | 3 | 4 | 4 | — | 730 |
| 24 | 7 | 11 | 2 | 10 | 13 | 9 | 5 | 1 | 5 | — | 3 | 489 |
| 39 | 25 | 12 | 17 | 13 | 31 | 13 | 10 | 14 | 6 | 6 | 21 | 531 |
| 34 | 20 | 7 | 7 | 3 | 11 | 5 | 3 | 1 | 7 | 1 | 2 | 394 |
|  | 90 | 53 | 48 | 26 | 50 | 22 | 18 | 22 | 13 | 18 | 21 | 742 |
| 29 |  | 76 | 55 | 38 | 32 | 18 | 13 | 9 | 10 | 7 | 4 | 1,053 |
| 7 | 82 |  | 20 | 37 | 26 | 10 | 9 | 9 | 5 | 2 | 4 | 584 |
| 41 | 274 | 144 |  | 261 | 203 | 177 | 39 | 12 | 1 | 11 |  | 3,148 |
| 46 | 28 | 34 | 50 |  | 125 | 57 | 15 | 13 | 8 | 5 | 4 | 1,012 |
| 66 | 11 | 20 | 13 | 63 |  | 53 | 51 | 21 | 6 | 6 | 5 | 995 |
| 31 | 70 | 67 | 155 | 157 | 614 |  | 298 | 48 | 30 | 8 | 14 | 4,719 |
| 74 | 74 | 52 | 36 | 57 | 309 | 190 |  | 204 | 175 | 26 | 18 | 4,486 |
| 07 | 210 | 102 | 48 | 134 | 456 | 133 | 604 |  | 425 | 148 | 67 | 7,390 |
| 51 | 128 | 78 | 72 | 125 | 491 | 266 | 597 | 647 |  | 69 | 47 | 6,185 |
| 16 | 338 | 123 | 63 | 141 | 552 | 155 | 364 | 678 | 198 |  | 379 | 8,198 |
| 77 | 552 | 368 | 113 | 221 | 1,042 | 236 | 412 | 321 | 101 | 414 |  | 12,425 |
| 22 | 2,094 | 1.308 | 795 | 1,451 | 4,354 | 1,475 | 2,623 | 2,123 | 1,075 | 828 | 706 | 58,569 |

Source: Arbetsmarknadsstyrelsen.

## Table 12

Regression Statistics: Data for Sweden during 1960–1966: Unsubsidised (A) and Subsidised (B)[1]

| Variable | | Intercept, regression and multiple correlation coefficient | Standard error of regression coefficient and of estimate | Partial correlation coefficient |
|---|---|---|---|---|
| $\log \alpha_0$ | (A) | −2.96300 | | |
| | (B) | −3.04800 | | |
| $\log E_j$ | (A) | .82949* | .04873 | .38600 |
| | (B) | .86576* | .04227 | .39045 |
| $\log L_i$ | (A) | .76954* | .05627 | .50106 |
| | (B) | .51169* | .03986 | .50244 |
| $D_{ij}$ | (A) | − .00062* | .00004 | −.53182 |
| | (B) | − .00057* | .00003 | −.53188 |
| R | (A) | .78945† | .28174 | |
| | (B) | .88874* | .20749 | |
| $\log S_{mij}$ | (A) | — | — | — |
| | (B) | .30837* | .01568 | .57390 |

[1] Alternative (A) corresponds to the results in Table 1.7. The new element added in alternative (B), $S_{mij}$, stands for the absolute number of beneficiaries from starting assistance 1963–6.
* Significantly different from zero at a level of confidence <.001.
† Significantly different from zero at .05 level of confidence.

## Table 13

Residuals[1]: Unsubsidised (A) and Subsidised (B) Out-Migration from Northern Regions −

| Region | (A) | (B) | Region's share in total subsidised out-migration 1963–66 in % |
|---|---|---|---|
| Norrbotten | −9.907 | −2.421 | 21.2 |
| Västerbotten | −5.204 | .897 | 14.0 |
| Jämtland | −3.061 | .339 | 10.6 |
| Västernorrland | −2.507 | 2.638 | 12.6 |
| | | | 58.4 |

[1] minus=− underestimation of actual out-migration
   plus= overestimation of actual out-migration

# List of References

Abramson, Jane A. *Rural to Urban Adjustment*, Ottawa 1968.

Andersson, Åke E. and Jungen, Rune, *Balanced Regional and Sectoral Growth in the Long Run*. Paper presented at the Tenth European Congress Regional Science Association, August 1970, London.

Bauer, Raymond A. (ed.), *Social Indicators*, Cambridge, Mass. and London 1967.

Berts, George H. and Stein, Jerome L., *Economic Growth in a Free Market*, New York 1964.

Blanco, Cicely, *The Determinants of Regional Factor Mobility*, The Hague 1962.

Cullingworth, B., *Housing and Labour Mobility*, OECD, Paris 1969.

Drewe, Paul, *Steps Towards Action-Oriented Migration Research*. Paper presented at the Tenth European Congress Regional Science Association, August 1970, London.

Drewe, Paul, *Toward A State-of-the-Region Report for Los Angeles, A Manpower Account and A Population Account*. Unpublished manuscripts, School of Architecture and Urban Planning, U.C.L.A., Los Angeles 1970.

Duncan, Otis Dudley, *Toward Social Reporting: Next Steps*, New York 1969.

Echenique, Miguel, *Demand for Human Resources in Puerto Rico*, International Co-operation Administration, Mexico 1960.

Emmanuel, H., Klaassen, L. H., and Theil, H., 'On the interactions of purchasing motives and the optimal programming of their activation', Management Science, 7 October 1960.

Eriksson, Kjell, *Flyttning Och Familjeanpassning*, Göteborg 1968.

Even, Alan, *Evolution de la population en Bretagne depuis 1962*, Centre Régional d'Etudes et de Formation Economiques Rennes 1969.

Fahlén, Olov, 'En Studie over den Interregionala Migrationen I Arbetsmarknadsstyrelsens A-Regioner' AMS, Meddelanden från Utredningsbyrån, *1* (1966).

Foote, Nelson W., *et al.*, *Housing Choices and Housing Constraints*, New York 1960.

Freedman, Audrey, 'Labor Mobility Projects for the Unemployed', in: Monthly Labor Review, June 1968.

Godschalk, David R. and Mills, William E., 'A Collaborative Approach to Planning through Urban Activities', Journal of the American Institute of Planners, *32* (1966).

Goss, Anthony, 'Regional Planning and Central Government', in: Town and Country Planning, *36* (1968).

Greenwood, Michael J., 'An Analysis of the Determinants of Geographic Labour Mobility in the United States', in: The Review of Economics and Statistics, *50* (1968).

Gremion, Pierre, *La Mise en Place des Institutions Régionales*, Paris 1965.

Gross, Bertram M. (ed.), 'Social Goals and Indicators for American Society', in: The Annals of the American Academy of Political and Social Science, *371* and *373* (1967).

Hägerstrand, Torsten, 'Migration and Area', in: Migration in Sweden: A Symposium [D. Haunerburg and B. Odering (eds.)], Lund 1957.

Heide, Hendrik ter, *Binnenlandse Migratie in Nederland*, The Hague 1965.

Jenness, R. A., *Manpower Mobility Programs, A Benefit-Cost Approach*. Paper delivered at the North American Conference on Cost-Benefit Analysis and Manpower Policies, May 1969, Madison, Wisc.

Johansson, Sven Ove, Olsson, Sören, and Rundblad, Bengt G., *Kvarvarande Och Avflyttade*, Göteborg 1969.

Katz, Elihu and Lazarsfeld, Paul F., *Personal Influence. The Part Played by People in the Flow of Mass Communications*, Glencoe 1964 (first 1955).

Lewis, William C. and Prescott, James R., *State and Municipal Locational Incentives: A Discriminant Analysis*, Dept. of Economics, Iowa State University, Ames, Iowa.

Lowry, Ira S., *Migration and Metropolitan Growth: Two Analytical Models*, San Francisco 1966.

Maisel, Sherman J., 'Rates of Ownership, Mobility and Purchase', in: Real Estate Research Program, U.C.L.A. (ed.): Essays in Urban Economics, Los Angeles 1966.

Mazek, Warren, *The Efficacy of Labor Migration with Special Emphasis on Depressed Areas*, Working paper CURZ2, Institute for Urban and Regional Studies, Washington University, 1966.

Meyers, Frederic (ed.), *Area Redevelopment Policies in Britain and the Countries of the Common Market*, United States Dept. of Commerce, 1965.

Mills, William E. and Godschalk David R., 'A Collaborative Approach to Planning through Urban Activities', Journal of the American Institute of Planners, *32* (1966).

Moore, Wilbert E. and Sheldon, Eleanor B., *Indicators of Social Change: Concepts and Measurement*, New York 1969.

Morrison, Peter H., *Implications of Migration Histories for Model Design*, Santa Monica, Cal. 1970.

Morrison, Peter H., *Theoretical Issues in the Design of Population Mobility Models*, Santa Monica, Cal. 1969.

Muth, Richard F., *Migration: Chicken or Egg?* Conference Papers presented September 1969, Cambridge, Mass.

Olsen, Mancur, Jr., 'The Purpose and Plan of a Social Report', in: The Public Interest, *15* (1969).

Olsson, Gunnar, 'Distance and Human Interaction. A Migration Study, Geografiska Annaler, *47* B (1965).

Olsson, Gunnar, 'Utflyttningarna från Centrala Värmland under 1880-talet', in: Neddelanden från Uppsala Universitets Geografiska Institution, Ser. A, no. 178.

Perloff, Harvey, 'New Directions in Social Planning', in: Journal of the American Institute of Planners, *31* (1965).

Raimon, Robert L., 'Interstate Migration and Wage Theory', in: The Review of Economics and Statistics, *54* (1962).

Rogers, Andrei, *Matrix Analysis of Interregional Population Growth and Distribution*, Berkeley and Los Angeles 1968.

Rogers, Everett M., *Diffusion of Innovations*, New York and London 1964 (first: 1962).

Rossi, Peter H., *Why Families Move. A study in the social psychology of urban residential mobility*, Glencoe 1955.

Rundblad, Bengt G., *Arbetskraftens Rörlighet*, Uppsala 1964.

Somermeyer, W. H., *Multipolar Human-Flow Models*. Paper presented at the Tenth European Congress Regional Science Association, August 1970, London.

Stouffer, Samuel A., *Social Research to Test Ideas*, Glencoe 1962.

*Tweede nota over de ruimtelijke ordening in Nederland*, Den Haag 1966.

United States Department of Health, Education, Welfare (ed.), *Toward a Social Report*, Washington D.C. 1969.

Vanhove, Norbert, De Doelmatigheid van het Regionaal Beleid in Nederland, Rotterdam 1961.

Wertheimer, Richard F., 'The Return to Migration in the United States', in: Inter-University Committee on Urban Economics (ed.), Conference Papers, September 1969, Cambridge, Mass.

Wilkinson, Maurice, 'European Migration to the United States: An Econometric Analysis of Aggregate Labor Supply and Demand', in: The Review of Economics and Statistics, *52* (1970).

Willis, Jeffrey, 'Population Growth and Movement', Centre for Environmental Studies, Working paper *12*, London 1968.

# Index

134

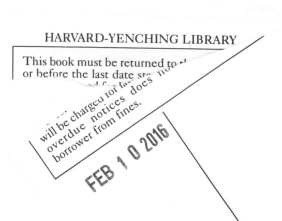